D0342841

Praise for Get Content. Get Customers.

"Pulizzi and Barrett have taken Integrated Marketing Communications to the next level with *Get Content. Get Customers.* The book includes how to combine old and new marketing, online and offline, print and electronic in innovative and useful ways. Every marketer, large or small, can use this text to build better on-going customer relationships."

— **Don Schultz, Professor Emeritus in Service, Integrated Marketing Communications, Northwestern University**

"Turning prospects into customers used to mean interrupting people with your company's product messages. But it was tough to break through the clutter. The Web allows smart marketers a better way: create compelling content that people actually want to consume. Pulizzi and Barrett show you how to create and deliver content and they provide dozens of examples of success to learn from."

— **David Meerman Scott, bestselling author of *The New Rules of Marketing and PR***

"Content marketing may be the most revolutionary obvious idea you'll ever hear ... that marketing works better when you actually have something to say. For those who are seeking to add a personality to their brand, this essential book will take you beyond white papers and give you a roadmap to making content a bigger part of all your marketing. Deftly navigating the worlds of PR, advertising and marketing — Joe and Newt prove that the real secret to great marketing is not a brilliant tagline, but creating compelling and useful content."

— **Rohit Bhargava, SVP of Digital Marketing at Ogilvy 360 Digital Influence and Author of *Personality Not Included***

"Joe Pulizzi and Newt Barrett take one of the core concepts of new marketing — that providing consumers with valuable content trumps bombarding them with irrelevant advertising — and give brands a treasure trove of tips, tricks, best practices and actionable approaches for using original online and offline content as a weapon in the battle for bottom line results. *Get Content. Get Customers.* provides a play-by-play for any marketer who is serious about breaking away from the pack, upsetting the status quo and moving beyond interruption marketing by offering compelling content that delivers real value for consumers and real revenue for their companies."

— Greg Verdino, chief strategy officer of crayon, LLC and marketing blogger at www.gregverdino.com

---

"*Get Content. Get Customers.* highlights the role content plays in making YOUR customers tick, click and stick. An eye opening book that takes you through a step by step strategy to enhance your content and to connect to your customers through words, pictures, sound and video. If creating great content that serves your customer and your customer's customer is important, this book is for you."

— Samir Husni, aka "Mr. Magazine"™, Chair of the Journalism Department, University of Mississippi

---

"When it comes to online marketing, you've got to reach people with what is desired and valued (content) instead of what is despised and ignored (advertising). Online, great content is effective advertising, and smart marketers are the new media. The trick to content marketing is getting your message across while keeping people engaged, and you're about to discover exactly how to do that with this book."

— Brian Clark, copyblogger.com

"As we rapidly enter the Post-Advertising Age, marketers are scrambling to find new ways to engage their brands with customers, amid the growing realization that the old ways are dead. If intrusion is dead and consumers are in control, *Get Content. Get Customers.* brilliantly manages the feat of combining the theory of engaging customers through content marketing along with alarmingly simple and practical approaches to doing it. All of this is clearly and intelligently illustrated through many different case studies. For marketers who understand that narrative marketing is the only marketing left but are struggling to understand how to do it, *Get Content. Get Customers.* finally offers the solution."

— Simon Kelly, chief operating officer, Story Worldwide

GET CONTENT.
GET CUSTOMERS.

How to use content marketing to deliver relevant, valuable, and compelling information that turns prospects into buyers.

Joe Pulizzi ▪ Newt Barrett

Published by Voyager Media, Inc.

Copyright © 2008 by Voyager Media, Inc. and Z Squared Media, LLC. All rights reserved.

Published by Voyager Media, Inc., Bonita Springs, Florida.

No part of this publication may be reproduced, stored in a retrieval system, or transmitted in any form or by any means, electronic, mechanical, photocopying, recording, scanning, or otherwise, except as permitted under Section 107 or 108 of the 1976 United States Copyright Act, without the prior written permission of the Publisher. Requests to the Publisher should be addressed to Permissions - GCGC, Voyager Media, Inc., 24600 Tamiami Trail South, Suite 212-352, Bonita Springs, Florida 34134, (239) 494-8597. Permission to reuse portions of this book is available through Copyright Clearance Center, 222 Rosewood Drive, Danvers, MA (978) 750-8400, www.copyright.com, email: info@copyright.com.

Limit of Liability/Disclaimer of Warranty: While the publisher and authors have used their best efforts in preparing this book, they make no representations or warranties with respect to the accuracy or completeness of the contents of this book and specifically disclaim any implied warranties of merchantability or fitness for a particular purpose. No warranty may be created or extended by sales representatives or written sales materials. The advice and strategies contained herein may not be suitable for your situation. Neither the publisher nor authors shall be liable for any loss of profit or other commercial damages, including but not limited to special, incidental, consequential, or other damages.

ISBN 978-0-9801878-0-9

Printed in the United States of America.

10 9 8 7 6 5 4 3

For Pam and Maxine, and to what is truly relevant and meaningful in life.

Table of Contents

Foreword

I f you're a marketer reading this book, you know that your world is changing. The seeds of those changes were actually planted nearly a decade ago.

In 1999, Google arrived on the scene and set in motion a sequence of events that would transform American markets and even American culture. By introducing technology that delivered information that its architects considered to be truly useful, Google began to change the language of business. Today, Google serves three-quarters-of-a-billion search results a day and stands as the Internet's universal homepage. That's a reality that successful marketers must embrace.

Marketing is moving online at a breakneck pace. Several research firms now forecast that the Internet will become the world's dominant advertising medium by 2012, or a mere 18 years after Yahoo! was founded. And if you believe that today's business users are online-savvy, you ain't see nothing yet. The next generation of consumers and business professionals that is now percolating in America's colleges and high schools spends 60% less time than their parents watching TV and 600% more time online, according to the Arthur W. Page Society.

At the same time, people are tuning-out conventional marketing at a dizzying pace. Today, your carefully crafted messages bounce off a wall of digital video recorders, pop-up blockers, spam filters, and digital music players. In the new reality, customers choose which messages to listen to and which marketers to let in the door. The days of what Seth Godin calls "interruption marketing" are over. The future is in "invitation marketing."

Customers have powerful new ways to reach out to one another. The population of the blogosphere skyrocketed from 1 million to 60 million between January 2004 and December 2005. Then, social networks exploded onto the scene, giving people the means to easily form groups to share experiences and rate the organizations they did business with. Emory University surveyed its incoming freshmen in 2007 and found that 97% of them had Facebook accounts. For the first time in history, people are engaging in a global discussion with others just like them—people they trust.

No longer can weak products be covered up by expensive advertising. Today, seven in 10 customers consult online peer reviews before making a major purchase. Buyers are engaging in discussions amongst themselves, and marketers are rarely invited. Years of shoving messages down the throats of customers who were helpless to talk back has denied them a seat at the table. They have to find a new way to get invited to the party.

That way is through content marketing, a concept that some people regard as new-age, but which is really as old as the village bazaar. Content marketing is about relationships and trust. It's about suppliers and customers forming bonds that spring from mutual dependencies and shared interests. It's about businesses really listening to their customers and endeavoring to deliver the goods and services that those customers need. It's about customers returning the favor by offering advice.

Many marketers are paralyzed by these developments. Business school taught them to analyze CPMs and response rates, not to engage in discussion. They learned marketing-by-Excel, not marketing-by-excellence. Some hope that content marketing is a fad, that we'll soon return to the good old days when conversations consisted of only one person talking. These people will soon be unemployed.

It's a Good Thing

Content marketing is actually the best thing to happen to the marketing profession in decades. That's because the barriers that for years have made marketers subservient to the media have fallen. No longer is it necessary to buy ads or to grovel before editors to get your message out. Today, marketers can *be* the media.

Search engines don't discriminate by source; they care only about the relevance of content. To Google, you are every bit as credible a source as the *New York Times* when your content is crafted appropriately. You just need to think differently about what you do.

This book is about marketing with content, which makes it an essential strategy manual for any company that hopes to compete in the new online world. Content marketing isn't about marketing in the old way. It isn't about intercepting and bothering prospective customers while they're doing something else. It isn't about intrusion at all. Content marketing is about getting customers to invite you to interact with them. It's about creating relationships that transcend transactions.

The few companies that are doing this right have seen remarkable dividends. Go to Willitblend.com for an example of a company that has used offbeat and entertaining viral video to convince customers of its products' superiority and drive sales up 400% in one year. Check out ClutterControl-

Freak.com or RoadWarriorTips.com to see how businesses can engage with customers by offering helpful free advice. These companies have a clue. And you know what? They're having fun too.

You don't need expensive campaigns or custom-built websites to reach customers. The secret of content marketing is to put yourself in the customer's shoes and look for opportunities to simplify and improve his or her life. It's about using the same words in your marketing materials that customers use in their search queries. The more in tune you are with the customer, the easier this process becomes.

Most of all, content marketing is about engagement. That's the dynamic by which companies find shared ground with their customers to solve problems. When you come down to it, that's what successful companies do.

This book is your guide to content marketing. The authors have years of experience helping companies establish and grow conversations with their customers. The case histories they present should inspire you. The arguments they present should challenge your thinking. The guidelines they propose should change the way you work.

We live in a world in which the old standards of competitive advantage no longer apply. Today, your best ideas are knocked off by your competitors and manufactured offshore at half the cost within six months. In this global and rapidly changing business environment, the only sources of competitive advantage are continuous innovation and outstanding customer service. America's most admired companies—Southwest Airlines, Dell Computer, Nordstrom, Progressive Insurance, Disney, Starbucks, and, yes, Google—build multiple two-way channels between themselves and their constituents. They listen till it hurts. They see their success as being wholly dependent on the success of their entire ecosystem of partners, suppliers, and customers. To these companies, conversations aren't artificial or unnatural. They're just good business.

—*Paul Gillin*
Author, *The New Influencers:*
A Marketer's Guide to the New Social Media

Introduction

Your job as a marketing professional is to get more customers to buy from you. It's that simple. This was true 50 years ago and it is still true today.

But you cannot get more customers to buy from you by relying on the traditional marketing approaches that worked 50 or even 10 years ago. Why? The Internet has transformed buyer behavior. Customers have access to vast amounts of online information from a broad range of sources. They can find almost anything they want in order to make an intelligent buying decision. They want plenty of information from you, too, but they want it on their terms. They expect to gather the information they need without being interrupted by unwanted marketing messages.

Because this behavioral transformation is so new and so dramatic, most marketers find it challenging to adapt. Yet there is a way to shape this transformation to your advantage. That's what content marketing is all about and that's why the content marketing revolution is on its way.

Content marketing is the art of understanding exactly what your customers need to know and delivering it to them in a relevant and compelling way. This extends way beyond the offering of product information and into the realm of best practices, case studies, success stories, thought leadership, and more. Once you have delivered relevant content, you become a trusted resource.

Content marketing enables companies to build a level of trust among their customers that makes it easy for those customers to buy. This is easy to say but hard to do because it almost certainly means changing the way you think and act about marketing.

How Did We Get Here and Where Are We Going?

Ten years ago, the Internet was well into its commercial phase, with companies of every size establishing some kind of Internet presence. Even so, the Internet was more of a marketing footnote than a marketing mainstay. Most buying decisions were still made the way they had been made since the 1950s. Print, radio, billboards, TV, and direct mail were the primary marketing vehicles chosen. They were chosen because they still worked. Publishing and media companies provided most of the content. Because consumer and trade media owned the toll roads, brands were forced to use these outlets as the middlemen in order to communicate with their customers and prospects. Publishing and media companies were healthy and profitable, and all seemed right with the world.

That is, until the Internet came along. Today, buyers and sellers can communicate with one another directly, without the need or assistance of traditional media outlets. Mass marketing is dying, and personal communication with customers is here to stay.

A perfect scenario, right? Well, not really, at least not yet. While media companies are suffering financially and even cutting back on their long-standing tradition of content creation, most businesses are still unsure of how to communicate with their customers now that the giant walls have come crashing down.

The Start of Something Great

While many organizations and some of the largest and most popular brands in the world continue to bang their heads against the wall of mass marketing, smart organizations have begun to do things quite differently.

These smart companies know they need to be something more than just vendors, so they've learned how to become significant content providers for their current and future customers. They've realized that they can be publishers and can fill the void of the faltering media. They've taught themselves to answer the call of this "new" Internet-age buyer. Slowly but surely, more companies are picking up on this idea that they cannot only create products and services for their customers, but also provide the information that will help their customers prosper and succeed.

Today, we're in the middle of marketing warfare. What began as a minor revolt against traditional marketing strategies has now become a full-fledged content marketing revolution. An irreversible shift has begun—away from media company-driven content toward content created specifically for customers.

Marketing organizations are now realizing that they can create quality content equal to or better than what many media companies are producing. Moreover, they are seeing that they can deliver tangible benefits to prospects and customers by providing relevant content that helps provide solutions to some of the toughest problems their prospective buyers are facing.

This type of content marketing benefits the customers of course. Customers love it. Who wouldn't? But what we are also finding is that content marketing drives revenues and may ultimately be the most important and effective marketing strategy available to successful marketing professionals.

Why Is This So Important?

All the rules have changed. You need to relearn the marketing game with a brand-new marketing mindset. Those who can adapt will flourish. Those who don't...well...think of dinosaurs.

Old-fashioned marketing is less and less effective with the new breed of buyer.

Unfortunately, most marketers have been trained to approach prospects with bold headlines, flashy graphics, and minimal text. We think of that as *billboard-style* marketing, or as more popularly coined by marketing guru Seth Godin, *interruption* marketing. Interruption marketing is still very prevalent in TV, radio, and print platforms.

In the days of mass marketing, interruption marketing worked very well. Your job was to hype your product while your prospect was engaging with a piece of wanted content or information. In an era of three TV networks, top-40 radio, and authoritative trade magazines as monopoly information providers, interruption marketing worked more often than not. Today, it's completely different. In a world of infinite informational choices, buyers will only stop for what's truly relevant and ignore the rest.

We live in a world where both consumers and business buyers want to make up their own minds about what they need. They search out and find the information they need to get their jobs done better or make their lives easier.

By the time customers are ready to talk to you—the seller—they are armed with information about your company, people, and products. This is true whether they plan to buy a Mazda or machine tools. It may not sound like it, but this presents a substantial opportunity for you and your company—an opportunity to educate potential buyers about your industry, possible solution choices, best practices, and the right questions to ask. Do this before they ever even call you or walk through your front door.

In this way, you have already begun a relationship that will make it easier for them to buy. That's what content marketing is all about. In essence, the customer has initiated a conversation with you before you even know they are interested in your products and services. Simply amazing!

By delivering content that is vital and relevant to your target market, you will begin to take on an important role in their lives.

This applies to your online, print, and in-person communications. And it's the same role that newspapers, magazines, TV, radio, conferences, workshops, and websites have played in the past. Now it's time for your organization to play that role.

This may sound like a pretty tall order. But we've gathered the essential knowledge, examples, processes, and how-to's you'll need to go from traditional marketing to content marketing, from interrupting to relevance. We've combined our decades of experience with that of the smartest content marketing practitioners on the planet to help you make this happen.

How to Put This Book to Work

We've written this book to simplify the process of developing and deploying a successful content marketing strategy. This is not a book about arcane marketing theories. It's a practical book about how to cope with new buyer realities. We provide you with an understanding of why content marketing is the optimum approach to cope with fundamental changes in the way your customers are buying. Perhaps, most importantly, we show you exactly how to make necessary changes with plenty of best practice success stories.

Here's what you'll learn:

» Why fundamental changes in the marketing universe demand that we become content marketing practitioners

» How to cope with the fundamental changes in buyer behavior by engaging in a dialogue with your prospects and customers that will make them want to buy from you

» How content marketing, executed properly, can accelerate the growth of your customer base, grow your revenues, and improve your bottom line

» How to really understand your customers, their concerns, and the best way to communicate with them by asking the right questions

» How and when to use the most important types of content to connect with your customers in print and online

» Best practices from organizations that are executing content marketing successfully

» How to develop a set of processes that will enable you to create, de-

ploy, and replicate effective content marketing strategies throughout your organization

» How to take advantage of a rich set of resources including check-
lists, online links, and a list of experts in various elements of content marketing

You don't have to read the book cover to cover. You may already understand
the importance of content marketing and just want the information on how
to make it work. Feel free to dive into sections that are particularly relevant
to your company.

You are in the middle of a content revolution, a revolution like none we've
ever seen before. It is simply the greatest opportunity businesses have ever had
to communicate directly with their customers. So, by all means, mark up the
book, turn down pages, and write notes everywhere. Do whatever you have
to do to put this book to work right now. ❖

Section One: Coping With the Content Marketing Revolution

Chapter One:
The Shift to Content Marketing

"We're not in the business of keeping the media companies alive...we're in the business of connecting with consumers." —Trevor Edwards, corporate vice president for global brand and category management, Nike, Inc. —*New York Times*, October 14, 2007

Nike, along with other huge brands such as Procter & Gamble, Johnson & Johnson, and General Motors, are all moving away from the basic advertising and sponsorship strategies that helped make them the well-known brands they are today.

That's a frightening proposition for both major media organizations as well as established brands. It's hard to fathom that the once-coveted marketing strategies that vaulted the best of brands to the top are becoming obsolete. Once you get over the initial shock that the world we live in has changed, you realize that this is perhaps the greatest marketing opportunity we have ever seen, both for brands in business-to-business and the business-to-consumer markets.

We are seeing nothing less than a marketing tsunami, which is affecting businesses of every size, regardless of what's being sold. Prospects are simply not responding to the kinds of marketing that have worked for decades. So most marketing organizations are asking, "What now?"

Beginning to Tell the Story

"We want to find a way to enhance the experience and services, rather than look for a way to interrupt people from getting to where they want to go," says Stefan Olander, global director for brand connections at Nike. "How can we provide a service where the customer says, 'Wow, you really made this easier for me!'?"

Olander's comment reflects buyers' increasing dislike of interruption marketing—those incessant advertising messages that stream and scream at people in print, on the radio, on TV, and even on the Internet—or essentially, anything that tries to take their attention away from the content they really want to engage with.

Big brands from around the world have realized that they need to market to their customers in a different way. The proof is in the dollars. The *New York Times* notes that "the 25 companies that spent the most on advertising over the last five years cut their spending last year in traditional media by about $767 million, according to *Advertising Age* and *TNS Media Intelligence*." During the first six months of 2007, those same companies decreased their media spending an additional 3%, or $446 million, to $14.53 billion, according to *TNS Media Intelligence*.

But those marketing dollars haven't disappeared. They are moving in different directions, many of which are content marketing initiatives, where money is being spent on custom magazines, newsletters, webcasts, content for websites, blogging, social content efforts, and more. In fact, *Publications Management*, a research-based newsletter covering the content marketing industry, found that over 25% of corporate marketing budgets are now being dedicated to some type of content marketing activity. And this number is growing. A recent IBM Global Solutions survey found that advertising executives plan to shift approximately 20% of marketing funds from impression-based advertising to impact-based advertising over the next three years.

Blendtec, a manufacturer of (you guessed it) blenders, has had tens of millions view its "Will It Blend?" video series over the last few years. The 30-second to two-minute videos show Blendtec founder Tom Dickson attempt to "blend" various items including golf balls, a toilet plunger, and even an iPhone. According to Blendtec executive George Wright, retail sales have increased by more than 500%, which he attributes almost solely to the video series. Talk about return on investment! With less than $1,000 and a YouTube account, Blendtec is now perceived as the undisputable blending king.

Smart marketers like Nike and Blendtec are beginning to understand that they need to be telling their own story. They are learning to create their own valuable and relevant content for their customers to join in on the conversation. They are also learning that it's hard to create meaningful relationships with customers through 30-second TV ads or radio jingles.

Nike's global sales have climbed in the last four years from $10 billion to more than $16 billion. And executives say this new focus on telling a relevant content story is a major contributor to that trend. In other words, content marketing has had a lot to do with growing global sales by 60% in a four-year period. Nike, through microsites such as its customer experience site Nike+, is not just talking at buyers anymore, but rather conversing with them.

You don't have to have Nike's powerful brand, huge budget, and global reach, or even Blendtec's creativity, to embrace a content marketing strategy that will grow your customer base and drive increased revenues. In fact, start-ups, small- and medium-size companies, associations, and non-profit groups are all benefiting from rethinking how they market their products and services. Just as Nike and Blendtec have experienced significant growth in tandem with the development of a content marketing strategy, so, too, can you deliver top-line and bottom-line results for your company.

How Many Names Can One Industry Have?

As you become a content marketer, it's important to realize where this industry came from. Many marketing professionals and publishers recognize the term "custom publishing," which, just in the last few years, has become the most popular term for the industry. John Deere is often credited for producing the first actual custom publication/content marketing device when it launched its newsletter, *The Furrow*, in the late 1800s. Yet, even though this industry is more than a century old, most marketers recognize it as young.

While we will adapt to any term that promotes business content initiatives, our research indicates that custom publishing is an often misunderstood term. Most marketers and publishers perceive that custom publishing mostly refers to custom magazines, newsletters, and other customized print initiatives, thus discounting the huge increase in online branded content. Actually, in a small research project we conducted with approximately 100 marketers and publishers in May 2007, most respondents chose to identify the delivery of valuable, targeted business content with the terms "content marketing" and "custom media."

Who knows which phrase will "stick" with people? Frankly, it doesn't matter. We chose content marketing because it seems to be the most understandable to marketing professionals. It's the blend of both content and the marketing of that content that enables customer behavior. But just in case, we've provided a list of relevant terms that are often interchanged for content marketing. You probably know a few more:

» Content marketing

» Custom publishing

» Custom media

» Corporate content

» Custom content

» Branded content

» Branded editorial

» Branded editorial content

» Branded storytelling

» Advertorial

» Private media

» Customer publishing

» Customer media

» Contract publishing

» Corporate publishing

» Corporate journalism

» Member media

» Info-content

Regardless of which name you associate with, content marketing is here to stay and may very well be the biggest opportunity your organization has to communicate with your customers like never before. ❖

Chapter Two:

Six Reasons Businesses Are Making the Change Toward Content Marketing

The shift to content marketing didn't just happen. It's been naturally progressing for years, ultimately reaching a "perfect storm" environment that sets the stage for this new kind of marketing. Here are six fundamental reasons why organizations are shifting, or must shift, their marketing efforts from interruption marketing to content marketing.

1. Change in Buyer Attitudes Toward Traditional Media and the "Credibility" of Content.

Today's Internet-savvy consumer looks everywhere for essential content in order to make smart buying decisions. In the last few years, buyer behavior has changed dramatically. Your customers are now increasingly knowledgeable about what they want to buy. They aren't surfing aimlessly, hoping to be influenced by marketing messages that arrive out of the blue. And they aren't sitting around waiting to hear from you. They have no time to waste, and they deeply resent unwanted advertising messages. In short, buyers don't want to be sold. They want to make up their minds based on their own information-gathering. Therefore, buyers need content that makes them smarter and more knowledgeable. Businesses that provide that content will win.

Moreover, as long as today's buyers get their answers, they don't care where the content comes from. They are open to learning from and acting on quality content, whether it comes from media veterans such as McGraw-Hill, NBC, CNN, or NPR—or from a custom publication, a newsletter, a company website, a favorite blog, or an RSS feed. That's bad news for traditional media.

David Levin, CEO of United Business Media, which owned the formerly-named CMP Media in the U.S., recently stated that "magazines as a vehicle for on-time delivery of news are clearly dead." (PaidContent.org, October 24, 2007)

This seems obvious as the just-in-time news outlets grow on a daily basis, but what is not as obvious is that the increasing number of news and informational resources are coming from businesses, and not traditional media companies. According to Alexa.com (February 2008), six of the top 10 most trafficked websites are either social media or branded-content sites such as YouTube. It is on many of these sites that businesses are marketing and creating their own content.

Search engines such as Google have democratized content to such a point that anyone with a little good content and a bit of search engine savvy can find their content on the first page. Buyers want information fast, and search engines help them get it.

All of this means that you have the opportunity to replace formerly vital media choices with your own high-quality content. You can be timely, considered, and reasoned. Your company can become the new thought leader among your many prospects who are completely open to great content from new sources.

2. Traditional Media Sources Can't Be Counted on to Assist You in Reaching Your Customers.

In the past, publishing companies drew strength from their unique ability to deliver target demographics on a myriad of definable markets. They invested millions of dollars in developing high-quality circulation that closely matched the marketing targets of advertisers. They were able to tell the advertiser exactly who read the publication, what kind of company they worked in, what types of products they bought, and how much money they spent each year on those products.

Just one look at what's happening in the newspaper industry tells the tale for the fate of traditional media. Daily newspaper readership has plummeted between 1970 and 2006, according to the Newspaper Association of America.

Age Groups	18-24	25-34	35-54	55+
Readership Decline	-50%	-55%	-39%	-15%

As of 2006, only 35% of 18- to 34-year-olds are daily newspaper readers.

November 2007 saw reports of continued drops in circulation averaging 2.5% for the top 538 U.S. dailies as reported by the *New York Times*. Some of the biggest suffered even worse declines:

» The *New York Times* daily circulation fell 4.51% to 1,037,828 and Sunday plunged 7.59% to 1,500,394

» The *Washington Post* was down 3.2% to 635,087 and Sunday was down 3.9% to 894,428

» The *Boston Globe* tumbled 6.6% to 360,695 and Sunday fell about the same, 6.5% to 548,906

According to IBM and the University of Bonn, 71% of consumers use their PC for personal time more than two hours per day, as opposed to 48% for TV. The trends continue to show that traditional vehicles are getting less share of voice, which means they will be less helpful in getting your message in front of your customers (regardless of customer behavior changes).

Do Marketers Know More About Buyers than Do Media Companies?

While magazines, newspapers, and TV offer less and less reach to buyers, disenchanted advertisers have built substantial databases of customers and prospects.

Smart companies of every size are using database technology to capture very detailed information about their customers and prospects, including all-important e-mail addresses. In fact, many companies today have much better buyer information in their customer relationship management (CRM) systems than do the publications trying to sell them advertising.

In fact, one of our former colleagues confided that a prospective advertiser had four times the number of qualified prospects in its customer database than the publication had in its circulation records. This four-to-one advantage left little incentive for the prospect to spend advertising dollars with this former colleague.

Within your market niche, you may well have access to more and better buyer data than your traditional media partners. You should consider targeting your database with focused content marketing efforts. That makes for a cost-effective way to reach and interact with your very best prospects. Eliminate wasted distribution. Create precise content marketing campaigns for well-defined sets of buyers.

3. Shrinking Media Company Budgets Reduce Content Quality.

Corporations often have bigger budgets and more resources to find and pay for the best research and content in the markets they serve. Unfortunately, too many media companies have been cutting both research and editorial budgets. Layoffs, pay cuts or freezes, and mass reorganizations are now commonplace within the traditional media environment.

Media companies in both business-to-business and business-to-consumer markets are facing a downward spiral in which reduced advertising revenues lead to cutbacks in editorial staff and editorial pages, and in the circulation size of their magazines and newspapers.

The decline in newspaper circulation, ad revenues, and staffing size is well-documented. Among the many reasons for these multiple, interrelated declines is the fact that young people have deserted newspapers for multiple venues on the Internet. Studies show that the average age of a newspaper reader today is 60, which in many cases is not the ideal demographic for most organizations.

In a 2005 post on the Newsosaur.com blog, Allan Mutter opined: "The decline in circulation, while no cause to rejoice if you love newspapers, could be a sign that publishers increasingly understand the need to scale circulation down to a core level of committed, valuable readers." He also warned that "shrinking circulation isn't necessarily a bad thing—as long as it stops *real* soon."

Unfortunately, over the last two years, circulation has continued to decline. In October 2007, Mutter said: "But the good news for publishers—that no one is demanding their liquidation any more—is also bad news, because it means they will be stuck tending to the massive and so-far insoluble problem of cauterizing the sales losses that have eroded profits at a quickening pace for the better part of two years."

As bad as it is for the giants—the *New York Times*, the *Los Angeles Times*, and the *Washington Post*—things are even grimmer for local newspapers such as the venerable *Akron Beacon Journal*, whose business section is gone on weekdays but survives on Saturdays and Sundays.

"We were one of the last papers to put the majority of stocks online. That's where the users are," said Bruce Winges, vice president and editor of the *Akron Beacon Journal*. "If I had my druthers, of course I would want a stand-alone business section. I don't think the quantity or the quality of our business reporting has gone down, but the perception of the reader is that they have lost something." (MediaLifeMagazine.com, October 17, 2007)

Continued Cutbacks Reveal Significant Opportunity

We could go on at length about the decline in traditional media outlets, but the real story here is the significant opportunity for non-traditional content creators to fill the void. Traditional media is suffering because the business models have changed, not because there is less information needed in the world. Actually, buyers need more information than ever. If Time Inc., the *New York Times*, or your industry trade magazine is not going to provide it, who will?

Businesses are beginning to understand today's marketing is a whole lot like publishing. The quality of many corporate publications and content websites today is excellent and ever-improving. If the trend continues at this rate, the quality of these vehicles will eventually surpass that of independently produced publications at some point in the future.

You have every opportunity to become a trusted content provider, even if you are a small company in a niche market. As media quality declines, look for the content gaps. Has your local business section disappeared? Perhaps, as a bank or insurance company, you could step in with relevant content. Have your favorite trade publications disappeared or lost quality? Fill the void with solution-oriented content that your buyers still need. Buyers need content. Be the new provider.

4. Selling to Your Customers Is Becoming More Challenging.

The more informed the consumer or buyer is, the more difficult it is to sell them. Smart marketers know this and are creating strong brand relationships by providing good, authoritative, even leadership-type content.

Great advertising still works. Think about the Aflac duck, the GEICO cavemen, or the legendary ABSOLUT vodka print campaign. These are all memorable and effective strategies, and, most importantly, have led to increased sales. The genius of the Aflac duck campaign for example, is that it is amusing, memorable, and still makes a very detailed case for why you would be smart to purchase Aflac insurance. Even in a very challenging financial environment, Aflac continues to grow revenues and profit.

Increasingly, however, the old-fashioned strategies are taking a back seat to content marketing in which companies engage in an interactive dialogue with prospects.

Paul Gillin, who wrote the foreword for *Get Content. Get Customers.*, points out in his book, *The New Influencers: A Marketer's Guide to the New Social Media:*

> "Traditional marketing and traditional media will always have
> a role to play in commerce. They will morph and can adapt
> to changing demographic trends. But it is clear that growth
> will be centered around conversation-based tactics. The next
> generation of customers will want to interact with businesses in
> very different ways. The new influencers are here to stay. Your
> challenge, and your opportunity, is in learning how to influ-
> ence them and becoming an influencer yourself."

As Gillin suggests, content marketing is all about engaging in a conversation with your customers and prospects. You can make this happen just as media companies have done for decades. For years, the best business-to-business and business-to-consumer publications delivered must-read content for the buyers marketers wanted to reach. These buyers, in turn, became loyal followers of the publications and responded actively to both editorial and advertising messages.

Although many media companies can't deliver on reader needs due to the evolution of these business models, readers/customers are still hungry for content that offers solutions to their problems—and helps them lead more successful, productive, and enjoyable lives. However, they are also inundated by thousands of marketing messages every day—and ignore almost all of these messages. To get through, you need to communicate differently.

You have the opportunity to transform the way in which you market by providing relevant content that positions your company as a trusted source. You begin as a source of information and continue as a source of products and services. It's neither necessary nor desirable to attempt to sell prospects who don't want to be sold. Instead, your thought leadership in print and online positions your company as the obvious source of solutions. As you become more customer-centric, you will develop an increasingly loyal and lucrative base of repeat customers as Nike and Blendtec have.

5. Because Technology Is Both Cheap and Easy to Use, Even Small Companies Can Deliver Great Content Solutions to a Targeted Customer Base.

Fortune 500 companies have long had the technological resources and investment capital required to build sophisticated content marketing solutions—and to manage huge amounts of demographic data relating to their prospects and customer bases. Many, such as Best Buy, Microsoft, and Amazon.com, probably know more about us than some of our relatives. They also do a terrific job of delivering relevant and compelling content to different segments of their prospect bases.

Smaller companies, however, have had to rely on media companies to deliver their message to their targeted buyers. This has certainly been true with print publications and, until fairly recently, online as well. Affordable technology is now changing all of the rules.

Just a few years ago, it would have been laughable to imagine that a very small organization could create and maintain a website that could be updated daily—and that would allow visitors to interact and even buy products and services. Today, it's not only possible, it's pervasive. In fact, a 10-person company may be able to out-market a 10,000-person company in a carefully chosen niche.

There are three core components underlying the shift in the technological balance of power away from media giants and toward companies of all sizes:

> » The ability to create sophisticated online publications such as websites, digital magazines, and eNewsletters

> » The ability to manage huge amounts of data relating to current and future customers

> » The ability to do both of these simply and inexpensively

A Sophisticated Website Cost $500,000 in 2004; $13,000 in 2007

Apple Inc. alumnus and serial entrepreneur Guy Kawasaki recently proved it. In an August 2007 interview for NPR's *Tech Nation*, he described how unbelievable changes in the price and usability of online technology had enabled him to launch a social media website for less than $13,000. Just a few years before, according to Kawasaki, it would've taken $500,000, months of work, and a big team to get the site up-and-running. Although the website, Truemors.com, may still be an unproven attempt at social media, it shows what any small business can accomplish. For example, the underlying content management capability would have cost six figures until very recently. Truemors.com is powered by the free blogging application, WordPress.

Low-cost, easy-to-use web technology now enables medium-sized manufacturers, small companies, or one-person service firms to build online content solutions that are more sophisticated than what most media companies were putting online just a few years ago. In fact, with focus, creativity, and a little outside help, these smaller organizations may be able to do a better job of providing targeted content to their best customers than some billion-dollar competitors.

Bye, Bye Middleman!

In the past, all but the biggest corporations had little power to target anyone. Sophisticated CRM software was expensive and hard to manage. Businesses relied on media companies because of their sophisticated circulation databases, which included lots of demographic information, enabling more precise targeting.

This meant that you could advertise in a magazine or you could choose a direct-marketing campaign to an important subset of buyers. In the early days of the Internet, media companies were also doing the best job of capturing e-mail addresses, which have become an essential part of any corporate customer database. So businesses would even rent expensive e-mail lists from magazines whose readers matched-up with their target audience.

Today, corporations and associations have created powerful databases that in some cases are better than audited trade publications and websites. Because the software technology required to manage a customer database is now affordable for any size organization (Highrise is less than $300 per year for a 5,000-count database), even small companies have less need for the services of trade and consumer publishers.

Moreover, there are plenty of online distribution partners, such as Digg, del.icio.us, and StumbleUpon, that enable you to reach well beyond your current database to prospects who are looking for solutions to their problems. Unlike most media companies, these new Internet buddies work for free.

The result: Affordable and easy-to-use technologies are enabling a broad range of companies to disintermediate trade publications and their media parents, because they can now communicate directly with customers and prospects. In doing so, companies are both reducing costs and increasing precision. Very importantly, effective and efficient distribution powers the very best content marketing strategies. After all, there's not much point in creating great content if you can't deliver it. Now you can do both.

6. High-Quality Editorial, from a Business?

The key to successful media programs for corporations is great content. Not just any content. Great content. Buyers know the difference between great content and a blatant sales pitch with no inherent value. Corporations can and do address this issue by, in many cases, establishing editorial standards that exceed those of some traditional publishing companies. For example, *Best Magazine*, from Best Buy, targets the company's very best buyers with high-quality content, rich in both information and design. Best Buy does not compromise quality with this publication, because its goal is to strengthen its relationships with those customers who invest the most time and money with the company year after year.

Conversely, media companies are often headed in the opposite direction. Media companies serve two masters: their readers and their advertisers. Sadly, as their ad revenues crater, they are caving in more and more to advertiser demands to compromise content, which shortchanges their readers. That weakens the editorial product, which ultimately results in lower reader engagement, lower reader response, and an ongoing downward spiral of ad revenues.

Of course, not every media company and not every publication has to make these compromises. But our own experience—and that of many former colleagues—makes it clear that this is an ongoing and almost certainly accelerating trend.

In a parallel trend, some of the best editorial talent has been forced out of media organizations to save money. In addition, hundreds of great editors are leaving voluntarily, because they cannot do good work within the content constraints of the struggling media companies. Many of the very best are moving to corporations where they are given the resources to create great content without severe budget limitations. Because smart companies understand that quality content is a key marketing driver, they are paradoxically less inclined to compromise in the way that formerly pure media organizations are now doing. Writing for Microsoft, Cisco, or Parker Hannifin actually looks good on a résumé these days. Not only can corporations afford to create high-quality content, but they are also attracting high-quality journalists.

Great content underlies great content marketing. Your buyers want and need great content. They used to receive it from media companies. Today, they can and should be receiving it from your organization. Even if you do not have internal editorial talent, plenty of brilliant journalists and editors will be happy to put their talents to work on behalf of your company. ❖

Chapter Three:
How to Develop a Content Marketing Mindset—
and Process to Match—Within Your Organization

Section Two: How to Put Content Marketing to Work

Chapter Three:
How to Develop a Content Marketing Mindset—and a Process to Match— Within Your Organization

The goal of this chapter is to help you develop a level of expertise in content marketing that will enable you to become an effective change agent within your organization. Specifically, you will need to develop a content marketing mindset, first for you and then for your organization. This will almost certainly require a major rethinking of your current marketing approach. It may not be easy, but it's essential.

By now you understand the irreversible trends that are changing the face of marketing. You also understand why it's possible for organizations like yours to think and act like publishers so that you can provide valuable content that makes you a trusted source for your current and future customers.

That's the all-important beginning to developing a content marketing mindset. But, because content marketing is a relatively new concept as it pertains to all media, it will not come naturally to you and your organization. Moreover, there is a skill set that media companies have developed over centuries that is probably brand-new to your organization. As you begin to think like a publisher, you will also need to learn how to create the kind of high-quality content that emanates from great publishers and great corporations.

Developing and executing content marketing initiatives that work takes time, effort, and expertise. It's extremely difficult to extract content from organizations that have no experience with content marketing.

Why the Reluctance to Move Away from Traditional Marketing Strategies?

Today, most companies are still using traditional marketing approaches that they may have been using since the middle of the twentieth century. There are several reasons for this:

> » Most companies are set up to sell products, not to provide relevant and valuable information to customers and prospects.

» Most companies have well-worn marketing paths that are easy to follow. Going off the beaten path into uncharted territory is intimidating.

» Most companies have strong relationships with media partners that may go back decades. It's not easy to break those relationships by pursuing a brand-new content marketing strategy.

» Many companies aren't measuring their marketing, so they aren't even sure what is and what is not effective.

» Many companies lack both the right people and the right processes to implement a new kind of marketing.

» Many businesses are reluctant to abandon traditional marketing tactics for what they may believe to be unproven content marketing practices.

» Most companies lack content marketing role models from whom they can learn best practices.

Or maybe you work in the kind of organization where no one even realizes that traditional marketing is no longer working. Perhaps no alarm bells have gone off yet.

In chapter Twenty-One, you will learn more about the innovative print and online content marketing efforts of British law firm Pinsent Masons. For all their success with content marketing, they used to be strictly traditional marketers too.

In 2000, they were still cranking out traditional brochures by the thousands. They were easy to produce, but contained the same boring, company-centric, feature-laden content that populates most traditional marketing materials. For the most part, business executives who receive marketing materials like these toss them out soon after receiving them.

Business development folks at the firm finally realized that they were spending money on something that no longer worked—if it had ever worked. So as part of an overall content marketing strategy, they launched a magazine that was designed to be read and to be valued by their target client base.

Making this change required the same kind of shift in mindset that will be required of all marketers from now on. It also required an investment in people, time, and processes. As you will read, Pinsent Masons has achieved dramatic positive benefits from the shift away from traditional marketing toward a multi-faceted content marketing strategy.

Chapter Three:
*How to Develop a Content Marketing Mindset—
and Process to Match—Within Your Organization*

Think Like a Publisher

As we have discussed, you must think like a publisher by delivering relevant content that will have intrinsic value to your targeted customers.

Bad, boring brochures are only part of the problem with traditional marketing. Fundamental changes in buyer behavior mean that advertising and marketing approaches that used to work are now ineffective.

The Yellow Pages is a classic example. Historically, whether you were selling consumer products or business products, you needed to be in the Yellow Pages. For a very high percentage of marketers, this is no longer true. Why? Fewer and fewer prospective buyers rely on the print Yellow Pages to find products and services. Instead, they are going first to the Internet to seek out both product and company information. On the web, the Yellow Pages must compete for attention just like everyone else—especially with a buyer's first instinct revolving around search engines.

This fundamental change in buyer behavior means that your most important investment will be a website and/or a blog that offers content that will put you at the top of the list of possible vendors. But this requires a completely different mindset than was required to run effective Yellow Pages advertising.

In a December 20, 2007 *Wall Street Journal* blog about whether advertising in Yellow Pages still works for small businesses, the writer quoted a recent study that said: "About one in five (21%) of respondents cited it as the source that produces the most calls from potential customers. Word-of-mouth is a close second, cited by 19% of respondents, and company websites are next, cited by 12%."

Here's what is really interesting about these statistics: Although the Yellow Pages came out number one, it was only slightly ahead of word-of-mouth—and company websites came in at a strong number three, not that far behind the Yellow Pages. When you consider that the respondents were all businesses with 25 or fewer employees, this statistic is even more meaningful. Many small businesses don't even have websites. That makes this third-place finish astonishing.

Imagine if these same small businesses were devoting their Yellow Pages advertising dollars to creating great websites! Imagine, too, that they were driving traffic to those websites through the use of excellent content and intelligent search engine marketing! You can be certain that what is already a good source of leads would be a phenomenal source of leads. Moreover, once the website is up-and-running, the annual maintenance cost is a small fraction of what Yellow Pages advertising would cost.

You can extrapolate the Yellow Pages experience across all traditional forms of advertising and marketing. The key is to develop a content marketing mindset.

Because we know that saying this is much easier than doing it, in Section Three we provide best practice success stories, and in Section Four, an in-depth case study that describes the process from beginning to end. But first, here is our B.E.S.T. formula, a simple way to begin your rethinking process.

The B.E.S.T. Formula:
A Structured Approach for Creating a Content Marketing Roadmap

We've found that even marketers who are willing and eager to move toward a content marketing strategy find development and implementation difficult. Because there are few roadmaps to steer organizations safely through this marketing frontier, too few are willing to make the trek.

That's why we've developed the B.E.S.T. framework—so that content marketing can quickly become part of your corporate DNA. The process is designed to make it easier to transition toward the creation of valuable and relevant content for your customers.

The B.E.S.T. formula for content marketing is a simple guide that you can use to develop and deploy a successful strategy. It also lets you take a critical look at what you're doing now, to determine whether you are mired in the swamp of traditional marketing malaise.

In a nutshell, the B.E.S.T. formula simplifies a complicated process. Apply it so that your marketing is:

Behavioral – Everything you communicate with your customers has a purpose. What do you want them to do?

Essential – Deliver information that your best prospects really need to succeed at work or in life.

Strategic – Your content marketing efforts must be an integral part of your overall business strategy.

Targeted – You must target your content precisely so that it is truly relevant to your buyers.

Use the B.E.S.T. approach for all of your online, print, and in-person com-

Chapter Three:
How to Develop a Content Marketing Mindset—
and Process to Match—Within Your Organization

munications. That's how you can play the same role that newspapers, magazines, TV, radio, conferences, workshops, and websites have played in the past. Now it's your turn to become the trusted source that persuades prospects and buyers to become loyal, long-term customers.

First Understand, Then Be Understood

You cannot hope to implement a successful content marketing strategy without understanding exactly what outcome you require. Equally important is an in-depth understanding of your targeted prospects. Only then can you craft a content marketing approach that will deliver more sales, more customers, and more measurable results.

The answers to these questions will guide you to a profitable content marketing strategy.

Behavioral

» How do we want the customer to feel?

» What effect must we achieve with them?

» What action do we want them to take?

» How will we measure their behavior?

» How will we put them on the path to purchase?

Essential

» What do our buyers really need to know?

» What will provide the most benefit personally or professionally?

» How can we present the content for maximum positive impact?

» What are the mandatory elements of the campaign?

» What media types must we include?

Strategic

» Does this content marketing effort help us achieve our strategic goals?

» Does it integrate with our other strategic initiatives?

Targeted

» Have we precisely identified the prospects we want to target?

» Do we really understand what motivates them?

» Do we understand their professional roles?

» Do we understand how they view the product or service we offer?

If it's not B.E.S.T., it's simply NOT content marketing.

By doing what's B.E.S.T., you can achieve measurable results!

*Going where few people have gone before—
to the implementation of a content marketing strategy*

The answers to these questions will help you define your marketing communications strategy. By taking the time and committing the resources to answer these questions, you will have the necessary information to create a content marketing plan that works. Integrating the B.E.S.T. formula within your organization isn't easy; but as you have read and will see through the best practice success stories, content marketing isn't just something nice to do, it is imperative to growing and sustaining a profitable business. ❖

Chapter Four:
How to Select the Content Types that Best Match Your Strategy

M any information vehicles can connect you with prospective customers, but they don't all work equally well in every situation. Therefore, it's essential to understand your choices—and when and how to use them.

Here are brief descriptions of some of your options. We've also included at-a-glance charts to show what you can expect to achieve based on the content marketing tool you select. Finally, we provide a quick best practice example for illustrative purposes.

You can find links to our examples online at the book's website, GetContentGetCustomers.com.

Print

Relevant, well-written, and well-designed print publications can make a dramatic impression on your target audience. Unlike a website, where visitors must find you, you have precise control over the outreach of a print publication. Print publications are highly portable and can be read anywhere (even with no Wi-Fi connection). It's important to note that printing and mailing costs require a significant investment that will certainly only increase over time. Nonetheless, if you create a terrific, well-targeted print publication, you can achieve measurable results.

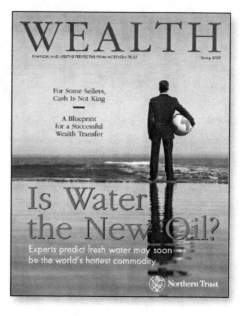

Why and When to Use Print Publications

	Custom Magazines	Newsletters	White Papers
Lead Generation			✔
Brand Awareness	✔		✔
Customer Education	✔	✔	✔
Thought Leadership	✔		✔
Perception Modification	✔		✔
Customer Retention	✔	✔	
Internal Communications	✔	✔	
Sales Support	✔		

Magazines

The magazines we enjoy the most are those that match our interests most precisely. This applies both in our professional and personal lives. So it is with magazines that you create for customers. You must understand exactly what information is most important to your target group—and the way in which they would like to receive it. In other words, you need to pay attention not just to your subject matter, but also to the style and length of the articles you write, as well as overall design and layout. Every element is critical to your success. Generally, custom magazines tend to be a minimum of 24 to 32 pages and are most often mailed on a quarterly basis.

Points to Remember:

- » High-quality editorial consistently delivered to a targeted database via magazine format

- » Generally 24 pages or more

- » Most effective frequency is quarterly or more

- » Some contain partner advertising to help defray investment

- » Be prepared to spend at least $40k USD for even a small initial distribution

Key Objectives:

- » Creates and maintains key relationships
- » Positions company as thought leader
- » Helps strengthen database efforts (use the direct mail list to update your customer database)
- » Can be your company's key sales tool
- » An effective way to bypass gatekeepers
- » Should also be used as an excellent internal marketing tool

Newsletters

Your newsletter may be just two sides of the page, meant to be folded and mailed, or it may extend to 16 pages or more. Whatever the length, newsletters are designed to be consumed quickly and should have attention-grabbing headlines with concisely worded articles. In terms of content, you must also focus on the precise information needs of your target audience. Beware: Too many newsletters are glorified sales pitches…today's consumers know better. Newsletters, due to their more timely nature, are often sent more frequently than magazines and should also refer customers to your website for more information.

White Paper Series

White papers focus on topics or issues that require a lot of explanation. They tend to cover technical topics, but may extend to any number of subjects. White papers are perfect for demonstrating thought leadership on subjects vital to your buyers. They aren't meant to replace sales collateral, so don't use them as an excuse to promote your products and services. Technical or not, they should be written in a style that immediately captures the reader's attention and pulls them through to the final paragraph. In other words, white papers need to be educational, but they don't have to be boring.

Points to Remember:

- » High-quality editorial delivered to a targeted database in white paper format
- » Generally between 8 to 12 pages
- » Can be targeted in print, electronic pdf, ordigital magazine formats

Key Objectives:

» Integrates with advertising program

» Creates a clear call-to-action

» Positions company as a thought/education leader

» Supports database efforts

» Can generate leads

Online

You have infinite reach across the globe when you establish a presence on the Internet. Even small companies can look like giants on the web. As Guy Kawasaki indicated (see Chapter Two), in 2007 you could accomplish for $13,000 what would have required a half-million dollar investment just a few years ago. Even better, once you have made your initial online investment, your incremental costs will change little, even if your traffic skyrockets.

Thanks to today's inexpensive and user-friendly web tools, it's easy to get started, to add an additional web presence, or to keep improving what you have. Many of these tools enable you to begin an ongoing dialogue with your prospects and customers that will improve both acquisition and retention. Smart marketers are getting better and better at putting the Internet to work as part of a cohesive content marketing strategy.

Why and When to Use Online Content Marketing Tools

	eBooks	Websites & Web Portals	Webcasts
Lead Generation	✔	✔	✔
Brand Awareness	✔	✔	✔
Customer Education	✔	✔	✔
Thought Leadership	✔	✔	✔
Perception Modification	✔	✔	✔
Customer Retention		✔	
Internal Communications			
Sales Support		✔	

Websites

Think of your website as your primary corporate presence on the Internet. If you are a small organization, it may be the only exposure you have. In that case, design it so that your visitors will be immediately engaged when they arrive. Make it easy for them to find exactly what they're looking for. You have less than

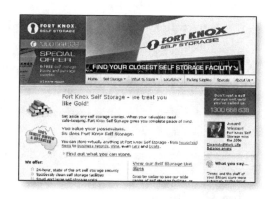

10 seconds to grab their attention before they head off somewhere else. Make it obvious how you can help your visitors achieve personal or professional objectives. As your corporate web presence, it must provide complete information about your company, the products and services you provide, and why they should buy from you. Be sure to use visuals that are closely connected to your written content. Mindjet (Mindjet.com) is a good example of a small company that combines content and corporate information effectively.

Content Web Portals/Microsites

Many larger organizations—and even some small ones—have multiple sites (or microsites) on the Internet. These typically concentrate on narrowly targeted area of content. For example, check out HomeMadeSimple.com from Procter & Gamble. It is P&G's content marketing web portal dedicated to solutions for the home. It offers ongoing original

content and a monthly eNewsletter, which has generated nearly 1 million consumer sign-ups. You may have also noticed that many large brands, such as IBM and Shell, are leveraging traditional interruptive media such as magazines and billboard space to promote their microsites.

Points to Remember:

» A microsite generally revolves around a key marketing objective/content area for the brand

» Often, the microsite is created with a separate URL

» Updated weekly at minimum

» Best practices include integrating it with a blog to keep the site fresh with new content

» Traditional marketing efforts are usually employed to promote microsites

Key Objectives:

» Creates an online community for customers/prospects

» Moves behavior through education

» Can enhance database activities and generate leads (in concert with eNewsletters and white papers)

eBook Series

When you have a strong body of knowledge inside your organization that you want to share broadly across the Internet, eBooks offer you the opportunity to reach out to customers and prospects. They in turn can pass along your eBooks to friends and colleagues. eBooks are typically 20 to 50 pages designed in landscape format with lots of bullet points and helpful graphics. An eBook can be created and distributed in chapters or as an entire book. An excellent example is *Small Business 2.0* from 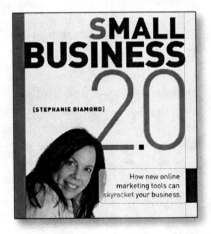 the Web 2.0 guru Stephanie Diamond (tinyurl.com/hszxm), as well as David Meerman Scott's *The New Rules of PR*, which has generated more than 250,000 downloads since its release in the beginning of 2006. Some eBooks are also chapterized and created as series, giving customers a regular dose of content instead of all at once.

Points to Remember:

» High-quality editorial consistently delivered to a targeted database in a chapter/book format

» Generally 20 to 50 pages or 5 to 10 individual chapters of 8 to 12 pages each

» Chapter eBooks should be at least monthly in frequency; weekly is better

» Can be a pdf or digital magazine

Key Objectives:

» One of the best lead-generation tools

» Opportunity for viral exposure and pass-along

» Positions company as a thought leader

» Helps strengthen electronic database efforts

» Educates customer/prospect base on key industry issues

Webcast Series

Looking for an interactive venue for content? Webcasts enable you to gather hundreds or even thousands of participants in a virtual room. One or more presenters deliver audio (or audio and video) content combined with a slide presentation. Partici-

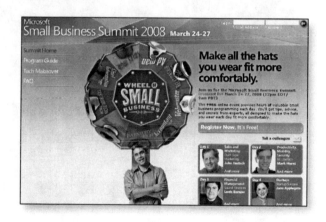

pants typically have the opportunity to ask questions of the presenters and have them answered in real time. Archived webcasts can be extremely valuable because they can reach prospective customers many months after the initial event. Microsoft is one of the kings of webcasts. Check them out at tinyurl.com/kdhv3.

Points to Remember:

» Web events can be co-branded with a traditional media company or sponsored individually

» Events are usually free to attendees, who must complete a registration form with qualifying information

» Events run approximately 45 minutes to an hour

» Webcasts through traditional business media outlets run between $7k USD and $40k+ USD; the average is $15k USD in business-to-business markets

Key Objectives:

» A powerful lead generator (sponsors receive all registration information from attendees)

» Brands the company as a thought leader

» Gets sponsor's products and services in front of key decision makers without sounding like sales

Why and When to Use Online Content Marketing Tools

	Business Blogs	eNewsletters	Digital Magazines
Lead Generation	✔	✔	
Brand Awareness		✔	✔
Customer Education	✔		✔
Thought Leadership	✔	✔	✔
Perception Modification	✔		✔
Customer Retention	✔	✔	✔
Internal Communications	✔	✔	
Sales Support	✔	✔	

White Paper Series

As noted above in the section about print, white papers are another way to provide thought leadership and deliver content that is vital to your customers. Even online, white papers tend to be very content-focused with relatively few graphics. Grant Thornton LLP does an excellent job of providing a targeted white paper series (tinyurl.com/3x6htg).

Digital Magazines

Today, you can replicate the look and feel of a print magazine online, delivering every bit of the brilliant design and colorful graphics that your print cousin can provide. In many cases, companies that produce print magazines now have digital versions online to complement them. This provides a way to integrate your print content with your web presence. Digital magazines combine the beauty of print with the interactivity of the Internet. They reside on, or are linked to, your website. Numerous software tools are available to create them. To see the possibilities, check out samples of digital magazines that Nxtbook has created at tinyurl.com/33vz4c. Marketers who don't like the confinement of a digital replica usually repurpose the magazine content via a microsite.

eNewsletters or eZines

These tools can be used to communicate regularly with current and future customers by supplying relevant content that's carefully targeted to their information needs. With an eNewsletter, typically you provide a brief paragraph or two for a set of five to seven articles with links back to the complete articles on your website. As long as you are providing valuable content, your readers will also be receptive to your request that they take action to sign-up for a newsletter or white paper. A good example of this is Tendo Communications' *Tendo View* (Tendocom.

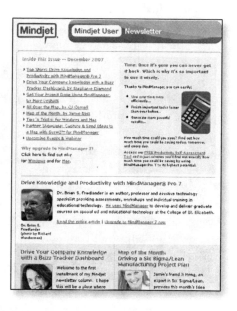

com/view). eZines are generally text-based e-mails that focus on one key story or concept. Shama Hyder produces an excellent eZine series at her small-business marketing site, AfterTheLaunch.com.

Points to Remember:

>> High-quality editorial consistently delivered to a targeted database via e-mail

>> Usually short, hard-hitting e-mail that links back to a web content portal

>> Weekly or monthly distribution

Key Objectives:

>> Create and maintain key relationships

» Generate feedback from customer base

» Tracked to show behavior patterns

» Can be a solid lead generation tool

» Consistently keeps you in front of customers

» Can be co-branded to gain third-party credibility

Business Blogs

Blogs—or "weblogs"—began as individual expressions of opinion about deeply felt topics or issues. Today they play key content marketing roles, enabling honest dialogue with customers who care deeply about your company, products, and content. Be sure to establish a blogging strategy that integrates with your content marketing strategy. Begin by asking the right questions: Why are you blogging? What will you blog about? Who will blog? Can you maintain frequent blog entries?

Can you accept negative feedback and respond openly and honestly? If you can answer affirmatively, business blogging could be a core component of your content marketing strategy. Check out Sun Microsystems' CEO's blog for a cool example (blogs.sun.com/jonathan).

A February 2008 Forrester study found that more than half of corporate marketers do not have a blog and are still trying to figure out the medium. The survey also found that three-quarters of all marketers don't see blogging as key to the overall marketing mix. This represents a huge opportunity for marketers who do see the value of blogging as essential to their customer communication programs.

Virtual Trade Shows and Conferences

Current technology and high-speed Internet connections enable the creation of lifelike happenings. Event managers can create Internet-based virtual trade shows and conferences to generate leads, increase event participation, drive revenue, and improve communication with current and future customers. To learn more about the technology, go to Veplatform.com.

Video Series

It's easy today to add video to your website, digital magazine, or eNewsletter. Video enables you to convey even very complicated content simply and convincingly. It also gives you the chance to humanize members of your team so that visitors feel as if they know them before they meet in person. As Blendtec has demonstrated, there may not be a more cost-effective or efficient way to reach prospects than with an interesting and creative method of displaying content through video.

Podcasts

A podcast is simply an audio file that you can listen to on your computer or MP3-type player. Often, podcasts are distributed as syndication feeds through RSS (Really Simple Syndication) or even iTunes. Podcasts are generally five to 30 minutes long, with longer podcast downloads becoming more popular. Paul Dunay, a marketing executive with BearingPoint, has a regular podcast series in conjunction with MarketingProfs on his blog, Buzz Marketing for

Technology (BuzzMarketingForTech.blogspot.com). Some corporations are expanding their podcast programs into video podcasts (vodcasts).

In-Person Content Marketing

Although the popularity and effectiveness of trade shows and conferences is suffering from cost pressures and the effectiveness of the Internet in some industries, most businesses still want and need to be physically in front of their target buyers. This is particularly true if you are selling complex, high-value products or services, where an in-person connection carries a lot of weight. Although live events require a great deal of work and a significant investment of both time and money, they will pay off if you make sure you target the right buyers and provide the right content.

Why and When to Use In-Person Content Marketing Tools

	Road Shows	Executive Roundtables
Lead Generation		
Brand Awareness	✔	✔
Customer Education	✔	✔
Thought Leadership	✔	✔
Perception Modification	✔	✔
Customer Retention		✔
Internal Communications		
Sales Support	✔	✔

Road Shows

Road shows are mini-conferences or tours typically conducted by a single organization, although related companies that don't compete will often participate. Usually, individual events last for a day or less, and are conducted in cities where is there is a high concentration of prospective customers. As always, it's essential that attendees walk away believing that they have received valuable, problem-solving information that positions your organization as a thought leader. Road shows often take the form of ongoing training for customers dealing with complex product issues. Large design software firms, such as Autodesk and SolidWorks, have been producing these types of events for years, and road shows have become one of their largest marketing initiatives.

Executive Roundtables

An executive roundtable is a gathering of industry executives who are experts in their field with enough drawing power to pull in your prospects. Through brief presentations and interaction among roundtable participants, you have the opportunity once again to position yourself as a thought leader. You will also be perceived as an industry force that can bring many key influencers together. The best part? Your customers will have the chance to learn and improve themselves and their companies—all because of you.

Repurpose. Repurpose. Repurpose.

Be sure to repurpose the best content that comes out of your road shows and roundtables. You will certainly have photography, transcripts, audio, and video from your in-person events that will serve as valuable content for magazine articles, newsletters, white papers, websites, podcasts, video podcasts, and other video productions. ❖

Chapter Five:
Making Great Content Happen

M any businesses, especially small businesses, may not have the financial resources to create a glossy custom magazine program, but all companies can initiate an effective content marketing program that works.

By using the B.E.S.T. formula from Chapter Three (Behavioral, Essential, Strategic, and Targeted), you can gather the information necessary to begin the content plan. Once that is complete, take that information and follow these four steps in detail to create your content plan.

1. Determine Which Organizational Goals Will Be Affected by the Content Program.

To be successful, an effective content marketing program must directly tie to your organization's overall objectives. Don't get into creating content because it's in style. Do it because it truly helps your customers and, in turn, your business. Here are some reasons we've actually heard before from marketing professionals who want to launch content programs:

» "We want to drive more traffic to our website."

» "Our competitors are doing it, so we need to do it too."

» "We'd really like to win an award for this."

» "We have tons of great information in this company—we need to tell the world about all the wonderful things we're doing."

Some of the above may sound reasonable to you. The problem with each of them is that they are not measurable and don't consider the customer for a second. How does driving more traffic to your website accomplish your organizational goals? Just because your company has lots of "great" information, does that mean that telling the story will bring you more revenue? Not in and of itself. Remember, the ultimate goal here is a behavior change.

Most of the key problems with a content program result from a clear misunderstanding of organizational goals. So, let's start there. Organizational goals must be two things: specific and customer-focused. Here are a few examples of organizational goals:

» Increase our number of domestic widget-line software customers by 20%

» Generate an average of 10% revenue growth with our top 20% of customers in Latin America

» Sell consulting packages to 10 new customers in 2008

These may seem simple, but it's amazing how many marketing organizations don't bring these types of goals to the table when creating a content program. So, before you launch your content program, be sure to list your key organizational goals. Once that is complete, understand which ones you are trying to affect with the online or off-line content program.

2. Determine the Informational Needs of the Buyer.

Most people want to move directly into creating the tactics for the content program. Makes sense for it to be that way, right? Now that you understand the organizational goals and have chosen the ones that will be affected by the content program, you can come up with some clear and measurable content marketing tactics. Right? Wrong.

Let us give you an example that is more personal. Let's say you want to shape your daughter into the next Tiger Woods. So, a reasonable goal would be for her to win the junior nationals. Since that is your goal, you create a plan-of-action that includes finding a personal golf coach for your daughter, signing her up for the junior league program, and buying her the latest in golf equipment. Sound reasonable?

Unfortunately, when you created the plan, you didn't consult your daughter (the customer) about what you wanted her to be—or what she needs for her success model. What if your daughter doesn't like golf? What if she likes golf, but doesn't want to be in competitive sports? What if she's built for basketball, or engineering? Worse yet, what if you were so busy planning the strategy, you didn't realize she was left-handed?

This may seem like a strange example, but this exact issue comes up in organizations all the time. Businesses create specific content so that customers react in very specific ways. Without a clear understanding of the customer's information needs, any re-

action that is close to the end goal is pure dumb luck.

Successful businesses already have a pretty good understanding of their core buyers. In order to create an effective content program, you need to take it a step further. Businesses with content marketing programs create content that is supposed to do very specific things. Just think how pointless this would be if you didn't know what information customers need to make better buying decisions—buying decisions that ultimately lead back to the organization's overall goals.

Understand your customers by doing comprehensive research. Comprehensive research does not necessarily mean expensive. Think of your research as including the following:

» Phone calls and in-person meetings with customers—include people that you think should be customers (what we call "shutouts")

» Zoomerang or SurveyMonkey e-mail surveys to customers and prospects

» Discussions with your customer service and sales personnel

By doing the above, you'll be able to create a buyer persona (a vision of who your target customer really is) and a true understanding of what information they need, which will effectively get you to your goals.

3. Determine What You Want Your Customer to Do and Why This Helps the Business.

Have you ever asked someone who owns a company what their website is for? Most answers are scary and revolve around the ultimate response, which is "because you can't do business without one." Even companies that believe their websites drive revenue can rarely define exactly how.

Content marketing programs are no different. Organizations create custom magazines, newsletters, microsites, podcast series, etc., for all kinds of reasons. Many know exactly what they do and are supposed to do. Unfortunately, many others do not.

Before you initiate and create the content for your content marketing plan, make sure:

» The content plan specifically drives your organization's goals

» The action(s) you want the customer to take is in some way measurable

» The content is based on your research about the buyers' informational needs

If you have each of these components, you can create very specific goals for your content program. Some of these goals will be easy to link to your overall goals (e.g., achieving a business transaction). Others will just be pieces of the overall pie that keep you going in the right direction. Examples of these may be:

» Downloading a white paper to extract more customer information

» Signing up for an eNewsletter or eZine to begin creating a relationship with a prospect

» Trial offer or demo that begins a conversation between you and the customer

Today, most organizations call these instances a conversion. Whatever you call them, make them specific and measurable in some way. Even print programs can measure conversions through group A/B testing and benchmarking studies, or specific calls-to-action that drive customers to web landing pages.

4. Determine the Product and Content Mix.

As we discussed in Chapter Four, there are a number of content products to choose from; and this list is growing longer every day. By mixing your knowledge of the customer, your organizational objectives, and, frankly, your budget, you should be able to determine an appropriate content mix of products. Remember, even though there are leading content products (e.g., a custom magazine may take the primary role), your content marketing program should be well-integrated with your website, microsites, ancillary content initiatives, and other collateral. Make sure all touch points speak to each another.

Now for the Hard Part: The Content

From our experience, the above steps are challenging but can be accomplished by almost every company in the world. Variations of these steps are used to determine customer requirements as they pertain to new product launches or product extensions, so savvy companies should be able to breeze through with no problems.

The real challenge comes at this stage, where we need to actually begin planning and developing content. The majority of organizations are set up to sell products and services, not to create and deliver consistently valuable editorial products. That's why the content execution seems so unnatural to most businesses.

Get Outside Help—Especially With the Content

According to the Custom Publishing Council, approximately half of all U.S.-based companies outsource a portion or all of their content activities to an outside expert publisher or journalist. Anything can be outsourced: project management, content creation, design, web development, audience development, distribution, marketing, and more. Of all these, the most important is content.

Many case studies are written by outside freelancers or editorial/content directors. David Meerman Scott, author of the book *The New Rules of Marketing & PR*, says businesses of any size looking to create great content have a simple solution: hire a journalist.

David states that "a journalist skillfully creates interesting stories about how an organization solves customer problems and then delivers those stories in the form of eBooks, white papers, content-rich web pages, podcasts, and video. And consumers love it. How refreshing to read, listen to, and watch these products of journalistic expertise instead of the usual product come-ons that typical corporations produce."

Let's face it: Marketers are so busy focusing on their products and driving demand that it's difficult to step back and think about customers' informational needs like journalists do. Also, great writing is an art form and takes talent. If you have that talent in-house, great. If not, find an expert from the outside. All companies, no matter what the size, may not always be able to outsource the complete project, but can always afford to hire a great writer.

The Editorial Plan and Schedule

Whether you decide to outsource your content or not, you need structure to consistently deliver quality content. If you think and behave like a publisher, you should create a content schedule that works from the present to about a year out. That doesn't mean you can't change things as you go depending on strategic objectives, product launches, or new customer information. What it means is that good content takes time. Whether you are creating content for a magazine, eBook, or video series, you need to plan ahead to get it done right.

Good content doesn't happen overnight. Most often, it takes research and revision to meet the needs of your customers. Therefore, two sets of plans are needed. First, create an ongoing editorial calendar with key milestones for content deliverables. Second, develop a production schedule for the project team to follow for each individual project. This is exactly what happens in traditional publishing companies. In order to keep meeting reader/customer demands, each product is timed to the day from every point in the process.

Where Does Content Come from?

The traditional route of creating content by completing a sound and reasonable content plan is always important. What's often forgotten, though, is that you can take advantage of content happening in and around your organization.

For example, do your executives and employees speak and give presentations on a regular basis? If so, get the rights to record them through video or audio. That's a piece of important content.

Do your engineers or process improvement personnel create industry documentation to substantiate designs or quality improvement measures? If so, rework it to create a piece of valuable content for your customers and prospects.

The list could go on forever depending on your organization. The goal is to look at what is happening in your company to uncover gems of content that can be reworked by your editorial staff and produced as original and valuable content.

It's a Process Issue

Jim McDermott, a publishing executive who spent 35+ years at Penton Media, Inc., continually stated one truth while he was a publisher and corporate director of quality at Penton: If there was a problem on a project, if there was a mistake, if the magazine was delivered late, if the customer was unhappy for some reason, if the content didn't meet the strategic goals…it was almost always as a result of a process breakdown.

In publishing, this is the ultimate truth. Delivering great content to your customers is delivering a promise to them. Once you start, you need to keep that promise. If a company has one or two content products, the schedule should be pretty easy to keep. But as more and more companies deliver integrated and multiple content initiatives to customers, keeping the schedule is a challenge.

Assign a Project Manager

Superior execution is the core of a successful content program. One person in your organization should be responsible and "own" the content initiative. Consider this person the "publisher" for your content efforts. Ultimately, this person is responsible for executing the goals you set out to accomplish.

When content programs fail, it's usually not due to a lack of quality content, but because of poor execution. That's why a project manager may be your most important content asset, even though this person most likely won't be creating any of the content. The project manager must ensure excellence in every content marketing tactic, including:

» Content/editorial

» Design/art/photography

» Web development/integration

» Content-specific marketing

» Project budgeting

» Contract negotiation with freelancers

» Print/web production and maintenance

» List/audience development and maintenance

» Research and measurement

» Responsibility for accomplishing the goals of the project

Sometimes, just a little upfront work can make all the difference. Such is true with content marketing. With a little planning, a few processes, and ownership within the organization, any size business can make an important impact in the lives of their customers.

Setting Up the Plan for Measurement

If you're going to launch a content program without any way or idea of how to measure it, stop right now. Content marketing and custom publishing programs have been talked down for years, much like traditional media, because of a lack of measurement formulas.

The great news is that content marketing can always be measured, if you have a clear understanding of your strategic communication objectives.

Just keep it simple and answer the question, "How will we know that the content plan is working?" This should lead you directly back to your organizational goals.

Return on investment (ROI) has always been dicey at best when it comes to marketing. The Holy Grail has been (and will always be) to link your marketing initiative directly to sales. Easier said than done. We've seen more than a few marketers determine ROI after the fact, taking whatever measurement they could find, to prove that something indeed worked.

Return on Objective

Perhaps a better way to judge the effectiveness of a content plan is to analyze return on objective (ROO). ROO was popularized while we were at Penton Media, Inc., in 2003 by Penton Group Publisher Bill Baumann. Bill, like the rest of us, grew tired of advertisers constantly barking about less than adequate ROI measures when it was impossible for us to measure sales lift—at least not without access to the advertisers' CRM databases for tracking purposes.

It was at that point we put our measurement energy into ROO, which was something that we could define in conjunction with our clients and use to keep both sides accountable. Before signing any final agreement, we would ask the question: "One year from today, how will you know whether or not the project was successful?" In most cases, we already knew the answer, but it was important to hear what the client said. The answer to that question was ultimately what we planned to measure…that was the return on objective.

The measurement of sales lift, impact, retention, etc., are key measurements to any ROO program. The "Measurement Picture" comes into play when sales data is missing or challenging. Sometimes ROO can be determined with one statistic, while other times four or five are needed to show an impact on the organization's business goals.

ROO measurements come in all shapes and sizes, and usually include multiple items to give you the complete answer to your question. The important aspect to remember is, it's not measurement for the sake of measurement. The tools and tactics below are used to directly answer what the project's objective is. If you keep that in mind, you'll get your ROO.

Here are a few measurement initiatives to get you started:

» **Tracking sales lift** of those who receive the content program vs. those who do not.

» **Tracking conversions** for online content products or print subscriptions, and measuring new or increased sales.

» **Online readership studies** to determine the impact of the content project, as well as the acquisition of customer informational needs and trends.

» **Measuring engagement** (time spent) through online research or by using analytic measures on eNewsletter or web portal products.

» **Pre-/post-awareness study** to measure the impact of the program. If possible, separate out a control group that does not receive your content initiative. Without that, it's challenging to tell if the project made the impact, or if it was something else in your marketing arsenal.

There are also a number of new online measurement tools that can give you some insight into how your content is performing, both with search engines and with customers themselves. Here are a few that you might want to check out:

Traffic Comparison Sites

» Alexa.com

» Compete.com

» Quantcast.com

» Trafficestimate.com

Blog Impact

» Technorati.com

» Icerocket.com

» Feedburner.com (blog RSS feeds)

Finally, here are some additional tactics to consider when integrating the "Measurement Picture" into your content marketing:

» Distinct 800 number on print and online initiatives

» Using individual URLs among different content projects

» Every print or web page should have some type of call-to-action

» Use print and online versioning tools to send more precise content to customers and prospects based on their individual needs, and measure the impact difference

Ultimately, we are only scratching the surface here when it comes to content marketing measurement. The key comes down to this: You have to plan for measurement. It is almost impossible to measure the content vehicle after you've already begun. An organization that invests in content without investing in the measuring of that content doesn't truly believe in the content initiative.

Don't forget these questions:

» What is the true purpose of the content marketing effort?

What are the underlying marketing objectives?

» What do you really want to tell your customers?

» Once you have their attention, what do you want them to do? What is the desired behavior?

» What vehicle best meets the needs of your customers?

» In order to meet your customers' informational needs, how should you integrate your content marketing efforts with other media? ❖

Chapter Six:
Putting the "Marketing" in Content Marketing

mar·ket·ing [mahr-ki-ting] —*noun*
The act of buying or selling in a market.
—Dictionary.com

Content marketing, taken at face value, is simple terminology for a complex process. *Content,* as in creating information that meets your customers' needs, and *marketing,* as in distributing and promoting it to a targeted group of people, inherently make sense.

This portion of the book is about all the ways to distribute and promote your content. But, distribute to do what exactly?

This book is not a marketing theory book, it's an action book. It was designed for you to take pieces and parts, and insert them into your marketing and content plans tomorrow. That said, it's important to understand why we are undertaking content marketing, why we are creating all this great content in the first place.

Go back to the definition of marketing at the beginning of this chapter. Marketing is all about behavior. It's an action. It's not about generating buzz, or website traffic, or press mentions—unless those things lead to profitable customer behavior.

Don and Heidi Schultz, in their book *IMC, The Next Generation,* state that "for all the complexity of marketing and communication plans, firms want only four outcomes from them." Those four outcomes are:

» To acquire new customers

» To retain and maintain present customers

» To retain and grow sales volume or profit from existing customers

» To migrate existing customers through the firm's product or service portfolio

What this means is that every bit of your content marketing focus must affect customer or prospect behavior. If this becomes the cornerstone of your content, the distribution and promotion of that content takes on a different meaning than just creating traffic or buzz. Every word and every page you create has a purpose: to drive the ultimate customer action.

Basic Principles of Content Promotion

Segmentation Is Key

Almost all businesses have different types and levels of customers. To be most effective, the ultimate distribution of your content should not be one-size-fits-all. Group your customers into different buying groups (also called buying personas), and treat both the content and marketing to them as separate.

Permission Marketing

Anything that you deliver to your customers or prospects that is not specifically requested could be considered spam. That is why it is imperative, for both your print and e-mail content programs, that you have your customers opt-in to your programs. Opt-in means that they have specifically requested your print magazine, eNewsletter, eBook, or other similar materials.

According to CAN-SPAM law, you have a right to use e-mail correspondence to communicate with your customer, as long as you have some kind of working relationship with them. But that doesn't mean that you can send them unsolicited information on an ongoing basis. Use e-mail information to get their permission to send them more. Use new offers to get them to sign up for your content. You must also give your customers the option to opt-out or unsubscribe to anything you send them as well.

Content Without Promotion Is Nothing

Lee Odden, one of the leading marketing bloggers in the country, posted this about the content vs. promotion debate:

> *"If you create great content and no one knows about it to link to it, you're spinning your wheels. A combination of content as well as social networking, link networking, public relations, and gaining editorial visibility as well as viral and individual link solicitations will all work together synergistically. Building a community of consumers of your content as well as relationships with the media in your industry is the distribution network necessary to gain the most link value out of creating great content."*

Almost all organizations believe they create, or can create, great content on a continuous basis. All too often, a brand will engage in a content project, not see positive results, and halt the initiative, thinking that the content didn't meet customer needs. The majority of the time, the problem was not necessarily in the content, but in the marketing of the content.

Meet Your Customers Where They Are Plus One

As we have discussed, your choice of media depends on your customers. You wouldn't necessarily roll out an iPhone digital magazine version if none of your customers had iPhones. That said, you need to help your customers take the next step. Yes, give them content in media they already use, but you also have to be cutting-edge.

Just because your research indicates that a small percentage of your customers engage in online video, doesn't mean you can't get them there. It's not like the iPhone example above, where they have to have an iPhone. If you create a valuable video on a topic your customers need to hear about, they have the PCs and Internet connections to get them there. As long as the content is truly important, you have the opportunity to be seen as an innovator just by the type of media you use to distribute your content.

Consistency in Communication

The old rule of thumb in print advertising is that it takes seven impressions of an ad per year to make an awareness impact on a decision maker. This is much the same with content marketing.

Behavior change doesn't happen overnight. Content must be delivered on a consistent basis in all media. That means one white paper should be part of a white paper series. One video should be part of a video series. One magazine issue does not a magazine make. Whatever you decide, send it frequently to your customers and stay on schedule. If you can't commit to a schedule, don't do the project. While great content can make a difference, going dark for a period of time or delivering it inconsistently will damage the perception of your brand.

Let Your Content Go

If you love your content, you must learn to let it go. In the past, brands had complete control over their content message and the medium. This is still basically true with custom magazines and newsletters. But the rise of the Internet and social media has changed the rules forever. Once our content goes online, it could end up anywhere. Let it. Regardless of where it ends up, the goal is to get that message out to the right types of people. If that happens and you see action, you've accomplished your goal—it doesn't matter whether they engaged in the content on your site or someone else's.

Why Does Marketing Content Feel So Awkward?

The majority of companies (yes, including media companies) that have been creating quality content for years never had to worry about marketing their content. They had targeted databases and targeted direct mail lists, and knew exactly where their prospects and customers were at most times. Today, customers can opt-out of just about every type of marketing they receive. Even though we may know more about our customers, they are becoming more elusive...elusive because they can choose to ignore our message at any moment.

Up until now, marketing time and resources have been used for brand advertising, sales initiatives, event marketing, direct marketing, and similar activities, *not* for marketing content. But today, since the average company spends a quarter of its marketing budget on content initiatives, it is imperative that organizations focus a large portion of resources on the marketing of it.

Mediaweek recently featured a story called "Is Social Media Killing the Campaign Microsite?" This brought attention to the fact that the microsite (or content web portal/content microsite) might be going the way of the 30-second spot. The author, Brian Morrissey, stated that "the growth of social media is causing marketers to realize they cannot expect consumers to always seek them out."

Social media is just one aspect of this issue. Ever-changing buyer behavior and expectations are another. Regardless of the reasons, custom content cannot be marketed the way it was in the past.

Let's take a look at the traditional custom publishing or content marketing campaign:

1. Create glossy magazine or newsletter.

2. Mail magazine/newsletter to targeted list of customers and prospects.

3. Upload content to the magazine microsite or newsletter page of website just before the print copies are delivered.

4. Repeat process in three months.

We may be simplifying this just a bit, but this is how 99% of the custom projects were produced. While this used to be more than acceptable, it just doesn't work anymore.

It's Not All About You

We've been keeping up with the postings from the folks at PandemicBlog recently and picked up on this review of an article by Kevin Nalts—one of the experts in viral marketing with video—on best practices for using viral videos. Kevin's thoughts struck us as so simple, yet the premise is something most content marketers have not yet realized. Kevin says:

> *"Would you go to Hersheys.com to watch funny videos? Probably not. Would you watch Hershey-sponsored videos via YouTube? Much better chance. It's based on when pharmaceutical marketers wanted their brand site to be the 'ultimate destination for people who have condition x.' Puleez—just go syndicate or advertise on WebMD."*

This is true for not just video, but for all your content that can be "webified." Heck, we're huge fans of the microsite. *The microsite is not dead;* it's simply just one way out of many that you need to connect and communicate with your customers.

Less Content, More Marketing

This is essentially the key, and there is no better example of this than in blogging. Successful blogging, to most people, is about frequency. That couldn't be further from the truth. Said best by Eric Kintz at mpdailyfix, blogging is not about "how often," but about how the blogger participates in the community. The same can be said for all your web content. However your company is involved in physical communities in your industry, you need to double those efforts on the web.

Right around the time we were finalizing this book, we had conversations with three industry experts—two marketers and one media professional—about their web content. None of them could figure out why they weren't getting more traffic. Outside of the basic search engine optimization (SEO) fixes, the majority of it came down to poor marketing, not poor content. When we asked, "How are you marketing your content?" it was like we asked them if they were the missing gunmen on the grassy knoll.

Here's the point: Before you create any more "great content," figure out how you are going to market it *first*.

New Media Promotion Strategies

As technology continues to change on a daily basis, so do the opportunities for marketing your content. Here are several promotion and distribution activities that you should consider integrating into your overall content plan:

Search Engine Optimization (SEO)

SEO is the process of improving your "organic" search engine rankings via Google, Yahoo!, MSN.com, Ask.com, and other similar sites. On a search engine results page, these are generally the results on the left side of the page (the right side is usually for paid listings).

One of the biggest reasons why companies are starting to pay attention to content is because content scores well in organic search engine listings. So, if part of your business strategy is better visibility within the search engines, you need to create a content strategy to create inventory for possible placement.

Content and SEO are tied at the hip. It's tough to have one without the other. As you launch your content strategy, you would be wise to work with an SEO expert to make sure you are getting the maximum exposure for your content through the search engines.

Search Engine Marketing (SEM)

SEM is generally referred to as the Pay-Per-Click (PPC) listings on the right side of a search engine results page. Many companies use PPC to generate conversions (to a direct sale, download, or free trial promotion), or to buy traffic when organic listings are non-existent.

Google AdWords and Yahoo! Search Marketing are the largest providers of PPC keywords. A PPC system is a live auction that updates every second, featuring those listings on the right that bid the most and score well (more clicks) for that particular keyword. Advertisers who purchase keywords only pay when the ad is clicked on, making the ad's effectiveness incredibly easy to measure when tied to an online event such as an online registration form. PPC is an effective method used to drive target prospects and customers to your white papers, eBooks, subscriptions or other content conversion pages.

Social Media Marketing

Content can play a large role in your overall social media marketing strategy. Social media sites can be broken out into Social Media Networks (e.g., Facebook), Social Web Applications (e.g., Digg.com), and even virtual worlds such as SecondLife.com.

Depending on the goals of the content program, and the target audience, sites such as Facebook and YouTube can be leveraged to promote your content initiative. For example, your company could launch a branded Facebook fan page where your employees can share content with customers on a regular basis. Regarding YouTube and other video-sharing sites, Blendtec has shown us that with the right message, video can significantly impact the profitability of a business.

Even though social media marketing is increasing its influence daily, most marketers are still just dabbling in it. This creates an opportunity for you to test which social portals provide the best return for your objectives and which sites your customers seem to be affiliating with.

Content Syndication—RSS

RSS, or Really Simple Syndication, is fast becoming a mainstream technology. RSS is a format that allows you to syndicate your web content to individuals with an RSS reader application or to other sites that wish to carry your content.

Organizations need to make their web content available through RSS feeds, including blog content, article content, and even news content. There are a number of services that provide RSS tools for free, including Google's Feedburner.com.

Leveraging Social Bookmarking Sites as Content Syndication Tools

Search engines such as Google, Yahoo!, and Ask.com allow each domain a maximum of two results on a search page. To dominate a particular keyword and receive more listings, you need to leverage social bookmarking sites.

According to Wikipedia.com, social bookmarking is "a method for Internet users to store, organize, search, and manage bookmarks of web pages on the Internet with the help of metadata. In a social bookmarking system, users save links to web pages that they want to remember and/or share."

Social bookmarking sites are generally used to drive significant amounts of traffic by people voting for a particular article (such as "digging" a Digg.com article). We believe that for most businesses, the benefits revolve mostly around search engine optimization.

Most social bookmarking and news sites receive high visibility with search engine providers. So, when you submit your article or story into a bookmarking site, that individual listing has an opportunity to be indexed by a search engine. The result: Depending on the keywords used, you could dominate a particular keyword with listings creating from multiple bookmarking sites.

Some of the most popular social bookmarking sites include:

» Digg.com (news)

» Propeller.com (news)

» Reddit.com (news)

» Mixx.com (news)

» Shoutwire (news)

» Del.icio.us (bookmarking)

» StumbleUpon.com (channel surfing)

» Furl.com (news)

» SmallBusinessBrief.com (small business/small business marketing)

» Sphinn.com (SEO-related)

» Junta42.com (content marketing)

» Hubspot.com (social marketing)

News Releases

David Meerman Scott's book, *The New Rules of Marketing & PR*, rewrites the rules for using press releases. The "new" news release is now more effective than ever. David's "New Rules of News Releases" include:

» Don't just send news releases when "big news" is happening; find good reasons to send them all the time

» Instead of just targeting a handful of journalists, create news releases that appeal directly to your buyers

» Write releases that are replete with keyword-rich copy

» Include offers that compel consumers to respond to your release in some way

» Add social media tags so your release can be found

» Drive people into the sales process with a news release

What this means for your content efforts is that news releases should be integrated into every part. If we recognize and understand that our target audience can find us today in new and unique ways, including search engines and social media sites, news releases become all-important tools in promoting our great content. This includes issue launches, cover stories, key case studies, white papers, eBooks, video launches, and more. Remember, the old goal of a press release was to try to get media coverage. The new rules of news releases tell you to promote your content so it can get found by the right people.

Putting the New Promotion Techniques to Use

Let's end this section by going back to the traditional custom magazine example. For the basic quarterly magazine project, here are some ways to get the most "bang for your buck" out of your content, and create multiple avenues for qualified prospects and customers to reach you:

1. Record audio and video of interviews for the magazine or newsletter for later repurposing (we'll use magazine for the rest of this example).

2. Develop a news release schedule before the magazine comes out. Target three or four key topics that affect your customers and the industry (based on the magazine content). The release link should take them to the magazine subscription or digital magazine subscription page. An incentive could be a free subscription to the print magazine or newsletter.

3. Discuss the magazine on your corporate blog. Get your editor to post some of the key findings/issues. If you don't have a corporate blog, create one on your magazine microsite.

4. Sent out news releases through a keyword-optimized service such as PRWeb.

5. Post videos of interviews to YouTube and other targeted video portals specific to your industry. Upload audio to microsites. Research podcast directories that may be relevant to your industry.

6. Print and mail glossy 32+ page magazine to your targeted database.

7. Send digital magazine version to the international audience or domestic audience you didn't want to spend printing and postage on (possibly a secondary customer target).

8. Make sure all articles have their own HTML pages on your microsite. Be sure each article has social media capabilities such as letting people add it to Facebook, Digg, or StumbleUpon, to name a few.

9. Be sure to Stumble! noteworthy articles and choose the proper

category for the article. Say, for example, the article goes best in agriculture; those people who have tagged agriculture as a key-word may see your article when they use StumbleUpon.

10. Provide something remarkable and different on your microsite for download. This does two things: 1) continues the conversation with your current customers, or 2) gives you information on prospects so you can begin a conversation with them. Something remarkable may be a free eBook about the 10 trends in your industry or a free white paper on a new, cutting-edge technology. Keep the sales pitch out. Seek only to educate at this point.

11. Use PPC, targeting specific keywords to drive people to your downloadable content offering.

12. Be sure to make RSS feeds available for your web content.

13. Continue the news release program, pushing the audience to the videos, an eBook, or key articles. Remember, news releases aren't for getting press; they are for building key links and for helping bloggers and influencers find your site. *Industry bloggers can be key to your magazine effort.*

14. Upload articles to key vertical and social bookmarking sites such as SmallBusinessBrief.com for small business, Sphinn for SEO/SEM, or Digg.com for wider exposure.

15. And if you are really on the cutting edge, create a Facebook fan page around your magazine or your company, and promote within that vehicle. Invite your key customers to join the Facebook group.

There is more that you can do, but this gives you an idea of how you should be marketing your relevant and valuable content. Think of it this way: How much valuable content have you or your organization created that has only been seen by one group of people—or worse yet, not engaged with at all? Marketing problem, not content problem. ❖

Section Three: Learning from Smart Marketers—
Best Practice Success Stories

Chapter Seven:
Best Practice Success Stories Overview

You may be surprised at the range of organizations that have implemented successful content marketing strategies. In the following chapters, we will examine how 14 organizations and three "solopreneurs" are using content marketing to connect with their customers.

These organizations range from multi-billion-dollar publicly traded multinationals to single-person companies run from bedrooms. Regardless of their size, you will find that the most important common threads are their customer-centric focus, a content marketing mindset, and a determination to create content that is relevant and valuable to their customers.

Although some of the success stories involve projects with huge budgets, others were undertaken with almost no monetary investment at all. There are key takeaways from every success story. No matter what the size of your organization, you will find ways to apply lessons gleaned from a fascinating array of content marketing implementations.

You will learn from a welding equipment company, a retail giant, a manufacturing media powerhouse, a bank, a chamber of commerce, a solo kitchen designer, an Australian web company, a British law firm, and many others.

Each organization has managed to bring an understanding of its most important customers to the creation of print, online, and in-person content. The net result of these efforts is a strong connection to customers new and old. Each organization has become a trusted vendor, based in large part on high-quality content provided consistently to their customers. ❖

Chapter Eight:
Yes, Content Marketing Can Make Welding Cool!

MillerWelds.com exemplifies how new-generation websites can deliver content that connects with current and future customers.

Type of Organization: Welding equipment supplier; subsidiary of publicly traded Illinois Tool Works.

Major Marketing Objective: To achieve an in-depth understanding of its customers so it can provide content that is relevant to helping them with critical welding-related issues.

Content Types:

» Print magazine

» Digital magazine

» Website

» Microsites

» Blogs

» RSS feeds

Unique Element: In addition to providing excellent content, the Miller-Welds.com website makes it very easy for customers to select and buy exactly the right products for their needs.

Results: Intense customer focus in the creation of broad-range content marketing underlies strong, multi-year, double-digit revenue growth.

Miller Electric Mfg. Co.'s powerful online presence shows that you can be both fun and informative. The company has a broad-based constituency, ranging from hobbyist welders to professionals working on skyscrapers, race cars, and airplanes. Amazingly, Miller manages to appeal to all of them online through its main website, several microsites, its blog, eNewsletter, and discussion forums. This is truly the very best of content marketing.

Miller was founded in 1929 to provide welding solutions at a time when blacksmiths were still earning a good living doing metalwork. It employs more than 1,500 people in its headquarters town of Appleton, Wisconsin. It also has an expanding presence overseas including offices in China. The company is a mid-range manufacturer that has been a wholly owned subsidiary of Illinois Tool Works since 1993.

Over the last three years, Miller has managed to achieve double-digit annual growth. The company might well have achieved this level of success without its leading-edge online presence, but those online efforts have certainly added significant value to its off-line efforts. Central to everything the company does is the need to understand its customers in order to deliver relevant content and, ultimately, precisely appropriate solutions.

As Vickie Rhiner, corporate marketing communications, emphasizes:

> *"The 'overarching' objective in all our marketing strategies is to understand our customer. Our research with the customer is what motivates us to provide information/content that is relevant to them. For many of our customers, the welding operation in their business is important to their very livelihood. As the manufacturer of the equipment they depend on day-in and day-out, they look to us for information that may help them with their most critical business issues, e.g., reducing welding costs, increasing productivity, operator efficiency, and equipment purchase justification (ROI)."*

You don't have to be involved in welding to get a feel for the enthusiasm that Miller exudes. One look at a recent cartoon from its eNewsletter will give you a pretty good idea: *"You know you're a welder when your welding helmets cost more than your car."* Miller's customers love what the company does—and the site reflects that.

Many online elements create a sense of community for several different market segments. At the same time, it's also obvious that this is a website designed to sell products and services.

At its best, compelling online content begins an ongoing dialogue with your best buyers from the very first moment they land on site. That's exactly what Miller accomplishes.

MillerWelds.com Is Anything *But* a Typical Industrial Website

As we will discuss in Chapter Nineteen (which focuses on ThomasNet), most industrial websites still fall far short of what's required to do business successfully in the twenty-first century. They simply don't provide enough information to make it easy to buy products and services. Moreover, most of them also miss the opportunity to provide content that enables them to build a trusted relationship with current and future customers.

MillerWelds.com is as good a website as you would expect to find from one of the major consumer packaged-goods companies. In fact, it generates a level of traffic that many consumer companies would envy—250,000 visitors per month.

This site and others like it are also beginning to take on the role that traditional trade and special-interest publications have played. That is, they are providing highly focused, intrinsically valuable content that helps their customers do their jobs more effectively—or pursue their hobbies with more skill. While their media company counterparts are suffering through big-budget cutbacks, they are pouring on the content steam.

Today, even small companies can offer their prospects and customers a rich experience with lots of content that is relevant to their particular interests. In this new generation, content marketing drives the online experience.

That is, by first understanding exactly who your customers are and what they need to know, you can provide them with content that leaves them smarter and more knowledgeable. Content marketing enables organizations of every size to attract and retain more customers.

Now That's Content Marketing!

Miller is well ahead of its peers in its understanding and application of content marketing. And, yes…it makes welding cool!

In fact, one of its competitors, Lincoln Electric, has a perfectly credible website. But, when it comes to delivering an outstanding customer experience, Miller beats them hands down. Although the Lincoln folks do provide good product information, at the time of this writing they weren't offering much beyond that.

MillerWelds.com provides customers and prospects with a rich, relevant, and fun experience by providing microsites devoted to welding applications and interests such as racing, manufacturing, and construction. Miller has made its website the "go-to" site for welding information. In so doing, it has become a company with whom you would love to do business.

MillerWelds.com has in more recent years become an information source for hobbyists and instructors. Vickie Rhiner relates:

> *"After Miller appeared on the cable TV show* American Chopper, *we were the recipients of calls, e-mails, and letters from instructors around the country looking for help with their welding curriculum because their class enrollment was soaring. Many of the areas you now find within our website are in direct response to what the customer has asked us for."*

At MillerWelds.com, it's easy to find information that relates to your particular industry or interest. For example, if your welding work relates to construction, you can find a dedicated microsite with a wealth of information, including well-written articles that will help you solve some thorny problems.

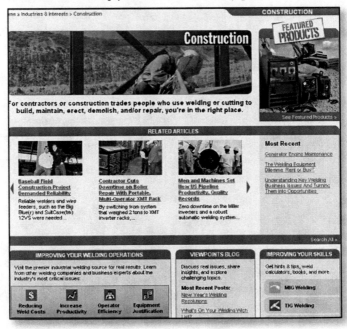

You can also browse an article archive by the particular problem you're facing. Thus, if you need to cost-justify an investment in upgrading your pickup truck-mounted welding equipment, the site tells you exactly how to do the analysis and provides you with a cost comparison that will justify the upgrade.

You can stay current on all new articles that are posted in your area of interest by signing up for the site's RSS feed. For example, if all you care about is the motor sports industry, you can sign up for motor sports information.

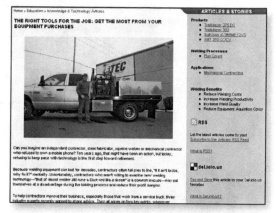

The Miller eNewsletter, *Power Click*, is another useful resource that directs recipients back to the website for even more information. The eNewsletter is carefully customer-focused, with only a small product item included.

The goal of the eNewsletter, according to Sue Feldkamp, manager of interactive marketing, is to "engage our customers and bring them back to the site often. We accomplish this by understanding what they are looking for and making it easy to find. Continuous evaluation of what they're doing on the web allows us to monitor and adjust content accordingly."

The Miller blog, Viewpoints, is prominently featured on the homepage. It's tagline "Visit. Learn. Share." reflects the spirit of the blog, in which the most popular posts draw dozens of comments. For example, posts that relate to solving the problem of the critical shortage of professional welders are both highly rated and much commented on.

Cool factor aside, this website is both comprehensive and easy to use. Plus, you can find exactly what you want to buy with very little effort.

But, that's pretty cool too.

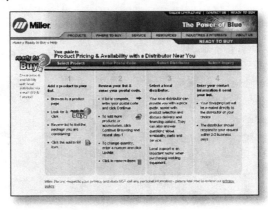

Since the company sells through a vast network of distributors, the "ready to buy" page is optimized for that process. First you select your products, then you narrow down your geographical location so that you can select the appropriate distributor.

What if you're not quite sure which products to select? There's a website solution for that too.

You begin by first choosing a broad product category that opens up a page that includes detailed tabular information which enables you to compare possible choices based on a detailed set of criteria. Once you make a possible selection, you are taken to a very detailed product page that includes everything (including the price). One of the multi-process products even has a page that lets you open a product simulator to show you exactly how it works.

Content Marketing Takeaways

Miller thoroughly understands this content marketing lesson: Although the Internet provides unique ways to connect with your customers, to make that connection, your content must be vital to their information needs while simultaneously serving your underlying marketing objectives.

If you deliver great stuff, you'll get permission to capture critical data (name, company, and e-mail address), and then to connect with your target buyers regularly. Regular interaction with your best clients will enable you to provide the product and service solutions they really need. By caring first about your buyers' information needs, you can then count on a growing stream of devoted customers.

The MillerWelds.com website reflects the passion for welding that the company shares with its customers around the world. By having segmented its website to appeal to both professional welders and hobbyists, the company demonstrates how well it understands its buyers. ❖

Chapter Nine:
Creative Content Marketing Enables a David to Compete Successfully Against Goliaths

There's a small hotel in a very nice place and it leverages online brains vs. big company brawn.

Type of Organization: Very small, privately owned hotel and resort company.

Major Marketing Objective: To dramatically increase reservations made directly from its website, rather than through travel agencies, to improve profitability.

Content Types:

» Website

» eNewsletter

» Blog

Unique Element: Strength of content is highly dependent on visual allure of the site, which turns visitors into virtual vacationers.

Results: 400% increase in online booking and significant profit improvement.

How does a small, charming hotel compete against corporate giants? Successfully, if you use the web as effectively as the 'Tween Waters Inn on Captiva Island. That's what sparked our attention in a September 13, 2007, article in *Gulf Coast Business Review*. Although we had actually stayed at the waterfront boutique hotel, we had no idea how smart its managers (and marketing partner, Noise Inc.) were about content marketing.

By fully embracing an online content marketing mindset, 'Tween Waters Inn has achieved dramatic bottom-line results through the use of creativity rather than the spending of big bucks. It has established clear objectives of increasing direct online reservations while building an impressive e-mail marketing list. This drops dollars to the bottom line, because the inn now pays only 6% commission on nights booked on its website—vs. 10% on various travel sites.

It's important to add that the team has been brilliant at using ongoing promotional efforts to create a very large e-mail list that is very receptive to its regular messaging. In particular, it has cross-promoted with a new airline, USA3000, to do joint list-building.

Southwest Florida is blessed with two beautiful barrier islands: Sanibel and its slightly more remote next door neighbor, Captiva. The 'Tween Waters Inn is a charming reminder of the gentler last century. But its current marketing needs are all about twenty-first century global realities.

Although it is a very small hotel (137 rooms and 19 cottages), the 'Tween Waters Inn is located in an idyllic setting. It is the largest hotel in the stable of its parent company, New York-based Rochester Resorts, so it lacks the national clout of the big brands and the big reservation systems. It is also at a local disadvantage because its nearest competitor is three times larger and just three miles down the road. In addition, 'Tween Waters competes with two Ritz-Carltons and a Hyatt resort less than 35 miles away. Of course, it also has to compete with the rest of Florida—Miami, Palm Beach, Orlando, etc.

With a very limited marketing budget of just 2.5% of revenues, 'Tween Waters can't outspend the competition—it has to outflank it.

Transformation of Old Website in 2005 Was Critical to Content Marketing Success

You have only a few seconds to capture your visitors' attention and persuade them to linger on your website. You won't make that happen without a combination of outstanding design and compelling content.

For a resort, the appeal of a website may derive more from how it looks than from how it reads. Visitors will want to imagine themselves as guests at the resort before they actually arrive. Elegant design carefully integrated with compelling content conjures up a virtual stay at the resort.

The resort's old website was fine for its time, but became inadequate as time went by. Because it was essentially unchanged since October 1997, it did not measure up to the standards of 2005. What was more than acceptable in 1997 looked very old-fashioned and out-of-date eight years later.

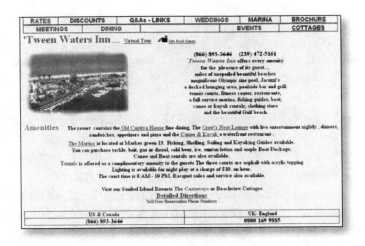

This is not to say that the website lacked content. In fact, all the basic content elements from 1997, such as information about weddings, the marina, meetings, and dining, have been posted at the current site. The website also provided a toll-free number front-and-center so that potential guests could call for reservations. However, what they *couldn't* do was book a reservation directly at the website. That became a major disadvantage by 2005.

What the 'Tween Waters Inn had going for it was endless charm and a perfect location on the Gulf of Mexico. It would be a wonderful place for a wedding. But the look and feel of the wedding page on the website failed to convey the sense of charm and beauty the inn offers.

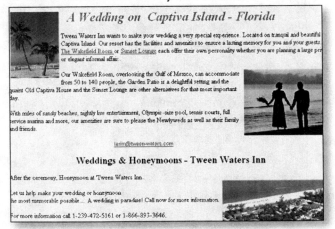

Back when the website launched, there was just one Ritz-Carlton Naples. The gulf-front Hyatt Regency Coconut Point had not yet been built. In fact, the Ritz-Carlton website in 1997 was mediocre at best.

But, in 1997, a compelling website wasn't all that important because most travelers were not using the Internet to plan and book travel. In fact, Harris Interactive research showed that only 16% of Americans used the Internet at home in 1997, compared to 70% in 2006.

Today, travelers surf the Internet before they do any actual surfing anywhere else. According to Pew Research, almost two-thirds of Internet users booked travel online in 2006. Therefore, a well-designed, content-rich website is probably the single most valuable travel marketing weapon. This is doubly true if you are a small, charming resort with a limited budget and very little national exposure.

Everything changed in 2005 with the launch of the new website and a creative, but inexpensive, marketing campaign.

Creative Content Marketing Trumps the Big Boys' Budgets

'Tween Waters Inn General Manager Jeff Shuff partnered with creative agency, Noise Inc., with offices in Wisconsin and Florida. John Sprecher, chief creative officer, worked with Jeff to brainstorm the new website.

The site captures the sensuous island feeling of Captiva and of the resort with 30 content-rich pages. The large, seductive images contain alluring text such as: *"The perfect place for the active enthusiast…or the enthusiastically inactive."*

But the 'Tween Waters site isn't just beautiful. It's designed to sell, with a reservation link on each and every page. Of course, it's also search engine optimized, taking advantage of Captiva Island's well-deserved reputation as a very special place.

The site is organized by both activity and event. Thus, if you are a boater, golfer, tennis player, or just a loafer, you can find exactly what's available.

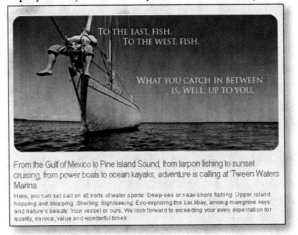

From the Gulf of Mexico to Pine Island Sound, from tarpon fishing to sunset cruising, from power boats to ocean kayaks, adventure is calling at 'Tween Waters Marina.

Here, you can set sail on all sorts of water sports. Deep-sea or near-shore fishing. Upper island hopping and stopping. Shelling. Sightseeing. Eco-exploring the backbay, among mangrove keys and nature's beauty. Your vessel or ours. We look forward to exceeding your every expectation for quality, service, value and wonderful times.

If you need to plan an event, 'Tween Waters makes it very easy to envision what's possible through the use of relevant graphical elements and well-written descriptions of the facilities and the staff's capabilities. For example if you're a bride-to-be, the delightful visuals will help you imagine what it would be like to have your big day on the edge of the Gulf of Mexico at a charming and intimate resort.

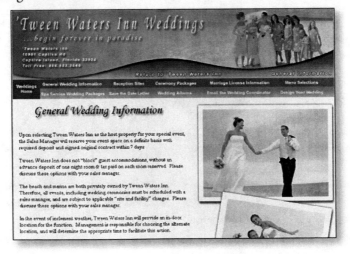

The Cost of the Website? Just $20,000. The Return on Investment? Priceless.

'Tween Waters Inn has gone from 5% online booking in 2005 to 20% online booking in 2007. The commission savings go right to the bottom line. Although the hotel doesn't share its financials, you can mentally calculate the positive profit impact of adding 4% more net revenue from all those online reservations.

"This year we're running 24% ahead in online booking," Jeff says. His immediate goal is to get 30%-40% of reservations via the website. (*Gulfcoast Business Review*)

This successful content marketing strategy continues to pay off in very measurable ways. This early twentieth-century inn has embraced very twenty-first century content marketing strategies.

Content Marketing Takeaways

You can successfully compete against bigger competitors who can easily outspend you, if you leverage every bit of creativity with your content marketing strategy.

For a travel destination, a great website with outstanding design and compelling content is essential. The quality of its website enables the 'Tween Waters Inn to compete successfully with much bigger hotels and resorts. Most importantly, the website is designed not just to look good, but to transform visitors into hotel guests.

You can create or recreate a strong brand by integrating online and offline marketing tactics. This integration dramatically increases the overall impact of your content marketing efforts.

By using customer-friendly ways to grow a large e-mail database, you can then communicate meaningfully and consistently with your best customers and prospects. In this example, ongoing communication strengthens the bond with guests, thereby increasing their lifetime value to the hotel. ❖

Chapter Ten:
Finally, a PR Agency that Understands Both Boomers and Blogging!

Genuine thought leadership from Fleishman-Hillard, built on blogs with personality and substance.

Type of Organization: Huge global public relations firm with highly focused internal practices.

Major Marketing Objective: Establish thought leadership through targeted blogs that make prospective clients smarter about, and more effective in going after, hot markets.

Content Types:

» Blog

» eNewsletter

Unique Element: These blogs have strong personalities that match their topics and target readers. They look and sound nothing like the corporate website.

Results: Fleishman-Hillard has been able to establish such strong thought leadership in its target areas, that it's the natural choice for companies looking for PR help in cracking those markets.

This global PR firm proves that you can use blogging to grow your business. Their people have become both boomer- and youth-marketing mavens.

Boomers Are Still Very Big Business

Baby boomers have been an incredibly important element in American society ever since they first showed up in 1946. As the oldest boomers turn 62 in 2008, they will begin having yet another seismic effect on the U.S. economy.

First they overcrowded elementary schools. Then they overcrowded Washington, D.C., with peace protests. And soon they may overcrowd the Social Security and Medicare systems.

Boomers were scary when they were young. They may be even scarier when they're older. One thing's for sure, they will continue to have a dramatic impact for decades to come. And they should almost certainly continue to be among your most important customers.

In the U.S., we tend to think of boomers as an American phenomenon. In fact, the population explosion occurred globally—in Canada, Europe, and the Asia-Pacific as well. Everywhere young men were off serving their country saw the birth rates soar when they returned home to begin long-delayed families.

For a global PR firm like Fleishman-Hillard, this offers the potential of global thought leadership. A highly motivated group of roughly 100 employees from around the world launched the "FH Boom" practice group in 2006.

Because Fleishman-Hillard had worked with AARP for years, it was clued-in to the association's research on the coming boomer tsunami. While most marketers mistakenly underestimated the looming cultural and economic impact of the baby boomers as they neared retirement age, Fleishman-Hillard did not.

Eileen Marcus of the company's D.C. office had a vision for a boomer-specific practice within the company. Partnering with Northern California-based Carol Orsborn, she launched the FH Boom practice. They understood that they had to break through to a younger generation of marketers who still underappreciated the economic impact and buying power of 78 million baby boomers born between 1946 and 1964. A blog would hit these skeptical marketers where they lived.

As Orsborn says, "We didn't want to start a practice that didn't have thought leadership, and it was clear that a great blog would be essential to help achieve it."

For content marketers of any age who are trying to stay current with the latest gyrations of this generation, TheBoomerBlog.com from Fleishman-Hillard is a wonderful place to explore.

Unlike so many of their peers who hide their thought leader-

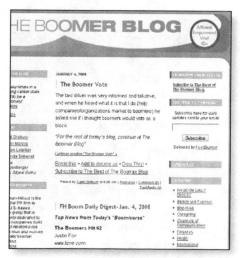

ship under virtual bushels, the Fleishman-Hillard folks are front-and-center with an enjoyable and insightful blog. They describe themselves simply and precisely:

> *"Fleishman-Hillard is the first global PR firm to offer a U.S.-based practice group that is exclusively dedicated to helping companies build powerful relationships with the men and women of the baby boomer generation."*

Blogger-in-chief Carol Orsborn is also the co-author of the book *BOOM: Marketing to the Ultimate Power Consumer—the Baby Boomer Woman*. Appropriately, she is described as a thought leader.

Carol and her energized team of colleagues use content marketing effectively to establish their individual and collective thought leadership on how to understand and how to market to the boomer generation. The blog is updated daily so there is always a reason to check in.

They also manage to integrate the FH Boom brand inside the blog with the "Daily Digest."

As they put it:

> *"This time, smart marketers, regardless of their age, are joining in with their own 'aha's,' courageously overturning the status quo that reflexively favored younger consumers in order to connect with our era's largest and most lucrative segment: men and women 42+.*

"The Boomer Blog is our solution, capturing our thoughts, discoveries, and growing intelligence of a multi-generational team as we grapple with, report on, and respond to the barrage of daily research, case histories, and news that is rushing to catch up with this fast-moving generation."

TheBoomerBlog.com contains loads of invaluable content on the "affluent, empowered, vital 42+" boomers, such as:

» FH Boom "Daily Digest" to keep marketers current on the latest in boomer coverage online

» Buying patterns

» The unique nature of boomer women

» Boomers and the printed word

» Case studies on successful approaches to influence/benefit boomers—much of this is very much content marketing

» Links to boomer-specific online resources

» The FH Boom team also reaches several thousand RSS subscribers who are receiving daily updates.

To contact:

Eileen Marcus
202-828-8886
marcuse@fleishman.com

Carol Orsborn
707-337-1064
Carol.orsborn@fleishman.com

FH Boom^{SM} Offerings:

The FH Boom^{SM} Training, Keynotes and Consulting

• Training for marketers, senior leadership and executives on connecting positively with boomers based on the latest research
• Keynotes, speeches and retreats on related topics

The FH Boom^{SM} Communications Inventory

A review process designed to analyze campaigns already existing or on the boards in light of our proprietary intelligence about marketing-to-boomers

• Identify overlooked possibilities and

The website's striking, somewhat edgy look was driven by the boomer members who had to convince the younger IT and design folks at the firm that a stodgy, boring look wouldn't be appropriate to appeal to Gen X or Y marketers. And it wouldn't reflect the vital, energetic nature of the boom generation.

While they are busy generating a treasure trove of insights on the biggest generation, the FH Boom practice within Fleishman-Hillard doesn't forget that it also needs to do some serious rainmaking. The blog provides a complete range of information on the services that FH Boom provides.

They do a great job of highlighting FH Boom achievements and capabilities. TheBoomerBlog.com definitely makes it easier for blog visitors and RSS subscribers to take the next step—to become clients. In fact, Orsborn notes that they can directly track new business from prospects who started out as regular subscribers.

Three Big Boomer Aha's

If you're marketing to boomers (and/or are a boomer yourself), you need to understand their social and economic impact. Here are three important aha's from Carol Orsborn:

» Eight out of 10 boomers are online everyday

» Eight out of 10 boomers say they have no plans to retire

» Most boomers have no idea how popular they are going to be with employers as the "baby bust" generation behind them leaves huge holes within organizations

Blog-Based Thought Leadership for the Youth Market Too

Illustrating that it understands the direct connection between blogging and thought leadership in multiple markets, Fleishman-Hillard also tackles the tech-savvy younger generation with its NextGreatThing (NGT) blog. This is the creation of Alan Rambam, who leads the company's youth marketing team.

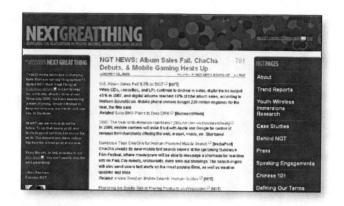

Here is how he describes what NGT is all about:

> *"Today's media landscape is changing faster than you can say 'blogosphere.' I started NGT at Fleishman-Hillard not just to keep up, but to stay ahead—miles ahead. Since July 2005, I've been assembling a team of young, dynamic thinkers to keep our company, our clients, and now you, in the know.*
>
> *"At NGT, we are curious about the future. To us, that means youth and technology—not just here, but around the world. Our research into Asian culture has become a focal point of our work."*

NextGreatThing.com couldn't be more different in the topics it covers from TheBoomerBlog.com, but it shares all the same enthusiasm, depth, and utility of its corporate cousin. NGT offers plenty of timely and insightful content, including trend reports, case studies, research, and an incredibly cool "Chinese 101" section. This is really great stuff.

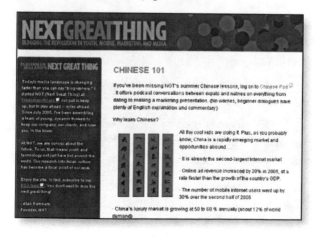

Yet again, Fleishman-Hillard has established thought leadership within a universe that is critical for marketers to understand. It has used a blog-based content marketing strategy to create thought leadership that ultimately drives revenue.

The Bottom Line

If you need to stay current on the "never say die" baby boom generation, TheBoomerBlog.com is the place to go.

If you want to understand youth culture, you need to hang out at the NextGreatThing.

Even better, if you're looking for a blogging role model, these are great ones to emulate. Fleishman-Hillard has precisely focused on illuminating supremely important markets. Not only are the blogs informative and insightful, they are also fun to read.

As Carol Orsborn sums it up:

> *"It is essential that our firm's people be perceived as thought leaders. This elevates all of our practice groups. We are demonstrating that we really do have detailed knowledge and that we are deeply committed to our markets."*

Content Marketing Takeaways

Giving away genuinely valuable content that helps potential clients market to boomers and to the millennial generation ultimately brings business to Fleishman-Hillard. As it has demonstrated, an informative, insightful, and interesting blog may be an organization's single best way to develop thought leadership.

Define a content area that will benefit from regular reporting and commentary. Provide plenty of substance. Don't be afraid to take a stand. You need to stand for something.

Make sure that your blogging team is passionate about the content covered. Be timely and update your posts frequently.

Make it easy for visitors to subscribe. Offer plenty of information that demonstrates your capabilities and encourages a phone call or e-mail to make the first step toward becoming a customer. ❖

Chapter Eleven:
Perfectly Targeted Content for Customers and Prospects

BookSurge employs two-stage content marketing. First, it makes it easy for authors to use its self-publishing services. Second, it helps authors market and promote their books.

Type of Organization: Self-publishing division of Amazon.com.

Major Marketing Objective: To attract and sign-up thousands of aspiring authors who need help with the many aspects of self-publishing.

Content Types:

» Website

» eNewsletter

» Webcasts

Unique Element: BookSurge aggregates and gives away comprehensive content on self-publishing success to would-be self-publishers.

Results: Because it is now part of a large corporation, the organization's leaders cannot disclose details, but admit that their content marketing strategy is working very well.

If you've ever written a book or thought seriously about writing a book, you may have some idea of how daunting the process can be. Of course, the writing itself is difficult enough—as we have come to learn. One really complicated part, however, is figuring out how to get your book produced and marketed. That's where BookSurge, an Amazon.com service, enters the picture.

BookSurge provides a complete solution for authors who are considering self-publishing but are clueless about how to do so. Not only does it provide a full suite of services, but also a ton of content that tells authors how to go about making their books successful. It provides that content for everyone who wants to take advantage of it, whether or not they ever become a customer.

Self-publishing a book is becoming much more popular today. Authors are realizing that publishing companies are not inclined to share the wealth—and because all but the most famous authors must do all of their own marketing at their own expense.

When you work with a publishing company, you might hope to get $1 to $2 per book at most. In a recent podcast, author Paul Gillin suggested that his successful book *The New Influencers* was essentially a loss leader because he was making so little money from it. He basically saw it as a marketing tool, rather than as a moneymaking proposition. I expect if he had it to do over again, he might well have decided to publish the book on his own.

Self-Publishing Can Turn Money Losers into Moneymakers

Self-publishing is not only respectable, but it can turn a money loser into a moneymaker.

In times past, if somebody said they were going to self-publish their book, you would probably assume that whatever they had written was so hopelessly bad that self-publishing was their only alternative. In addition, from time immemorial there have been vanity publishers who charged lots of money to print many copies of the book that nobody but your family members and very best friends would ever read. Today, there is also another breed of "self-publishing" company that really exploits authors by charging them lots of money and offering them only empty promises. Worst of all, many of these companies hold the copyright to the books in question, which leaves the book languishing for the length of the contract.

There is a better way. That's what real self-publishing is all about—and that's where a company like BookSurge can add real value.

If you self-publish, you can expect to net perhaps $7 to $10 per book, depending on a number of variables. This assumes that you would use the print-on-demand (POD) publishing model, which enables one-book-at-a-time printing. POD publishing means that you never have to be stuck with a garage full of unsold books. It also means that your upfront costs can be as low as several hundred dollars.

Moreover, as the nature of book selling changes and as the number of bookstores shrinks, most authors today will wind-up selling most of their books online or through non-traditional sources. This makes POD publishing the most cost-effective method for all but the biggest-selling authors. In effect, your book is always in stock because it can be printed overnight.

There is a possible downside for many authors. Self-publishing also means that you must operate as a publishing company, handling everything from copy editing to design to printing—and, of course, marketing. In effect, you have chosen to run a micro-publishing business. For right-brain writer types, this is not an appealing idea. Even worse, the idea of being responsible for marketing is very intimidating for many introverted writers. We recently spoke with an author who is a successful reporter for a big-city newspaper. When we asked her how her marketing efforts were going, she replied that marketing was the last thing in the world she was capable of doing—and that she just hoped to heck that her book would sell.

Filling in the Self-Publishing Blanks

Although BookSurge is not the least expensive POD alternative, it is a sensible choice for authors who need a real partner in bringing a book to market.

For a sliding scale of fees, BookSurge will handle most of those chores. They enable authors to turn their words into a finished publication and have it printed on demand. Whether you have a finished PDF version of your book that is completely designed and ready to go to press—or if you simply have a manuscript in Microsoft Word that needs complete editing and design services, BookSurge can create your finished book, prepare it for sale on Amazon.com, or hand it over for you to sell on your own.

BookSurge goes much further than simply handling book production details. Its team works very hard to teach you how to promote and market your book so that it has the maximum chance for success.

An Easy-to-Use Website

The BookSurge website makes it easy for potential self-publishing authors to decide to do business with the company.

When you arrive at the BookSurge.com homepage, you will quickly see what the company does and how it can help you. You can follow a logical process to understand exactly what services it provides and how much those services cost. There are no surprises.

You are immediately introduced to the "four easy steps" to self-publishing. You also learn that BookSurge is a company founded by writers and that it allows you as an author to retain full content rights. This means that should your book be picked up by a major publisher—or should you decide based on fast-growing sales that you want to manage your own printing—you are free to take the book with you. You also know from the header at the top of your browser that "*BookSurge is part of the Amazon group of companies.*" In other words, you can trust them.

Perhaps you're not ready to sign-up with BookSurge—and perhaps you never will. That's okay too. You can still sign-up for its newsletter. You can still attend its free monthly webinars. You can still learn a lot about the ins and outs of self-publishing by exploring the website. Thus, although Book-Surge makes it easy to decide to become a customer, it doesn't force the issue. It's obvious that the company is willing to take time to earn your trust before asking you to take any purchase action.

BookSurge is executing one of the best uses of content marketing. Even if BookSurge doesn't sign a customer up the first time, by offering high-quality content and getting prospects to sign-up for it, BookSurge now knows who the prospects are. From that point, it can use its expert content to create long-term relationships with prospects and ultimately reel them in as customers.

A Genuine Understanding of Authors

Content marketing at BookSurge reflects a deep and genuine understanding of authors and their needs.

As General Manager David Symonds stresses, "We think of our authors first…our job is to keep thinking of new and innovative ways to help authors sell their books."

The BookSurge eNewsletter is a perfect example of content marketing done exactly right.

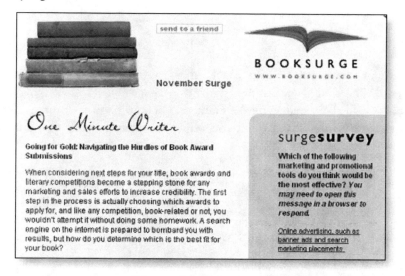

The genius of the BookSurge eNewsletter is its clear understanding of the concerns current and future authors have when it comes to creating a successful book.

A recent edition of the newsletter leads with a great story about how to submit your masterpiece for book awards and literary competitions. Those are things that authors absolutely need to know, but would have trouble figuring out on their own. There are also links to upcoming awards for which authors can compete.

To the right of the lead story is a quick survey, which asks, "*Which of the following marketing and promotional tools do you think would be the most effective?*"

This is a great way to determine the knowledge level and interests of authors who might consider using BookSurge. The folks at BookSurge obviously want to get to know their prospects and customers much better.

Scrolling down, you find that BookSurge is also offering a free webinar entitled, "Mine Your Own Business: How to Manage Your Product Line." The webinar is all about managing the marketing of your book to ensure its long-term success. If you're an author, you would not want to miss this webinar.

Kamilla Reid's Questory for Success

Inspiration can come from many places, but for Kamilla Reid, her 'aha!' moment came while watching the CBS reality series, 'The Amazing Race.' The concept for her series, *The Questory of Root Karbunkulus*, had been forming for some time, but it was as she watched participants of the race compete and perform challenges that the land of Dréamm became her reality. But, writing and publishing is not new terrain for Reid; having published her first fiction story at the age of eight and written and directed over 40 plays for the stage, Reid has spent the better part of her life bringing the "fantastic" to life in print.

Her vision for the first installment of the series, *The Questory of Root Karbunkulus: Item One: Mila*, was highly specific, and Kamilla recognized that, as a first-time novelist, by self-publishing her work, she would experience the same level of customer support with more creative control than with a traditional publisher. After investigating the ins and outs of self-publishing, she decided that BookSurge was a good fit, offering the best value for her book to achieve her goals.

Finally, you get to the sort of thing that keeps all authors from giving up—a great success story. Kamilla Reid had written plays but never a book. Inspired by the CV and CBS TV show, *The Amazing Race*, she wrote the first of a series of fantasy novels aimed at kids 10 and up. Unlike many writers, she's also a great marketer. She says: "In addition to an entertaining book, I knew I needed a great website and book trailer, all the things that I thought kids would love." Her highly interactive website, RootKarbunkulus.com, includes videos for ardent fans and a lively web forum. For more information about Kamilla, see Chapter Twelve.

The BookSurge eNewsletter is terrific because it really understands its readers: authors who desperately want to have successful books. There is almost nothing in the newsletter about BookSurge itself. Instead it offers guidance, role models, and great links that will inspire authors to keep on writing and keep on promoting.

Content Marketing Takeaways

BookSurge uses content marketing effectively to take a host of authors under its wing. Because it understands its target market so well, BookSurge succeeds with a website that makes it very easy for authors to make a positive buying decision. And even if authors aren't ready to buy today, they are likely to keep coming back for webinars, to read success stories, or to check out the latest tips in the eNewsletter.

It's worth noting once again that BookSurge's content marketing efforts succeed not because it is part of a company with more money than Warren Buffett, but because it understands its target customers and uses that understanding to develop relevant content.

There is nothing that BookSurge is doing on its website, in its webinars, or with its eNewsletter that much smaller organizations couldn't do with limited marketing dollars. ❖

A note on a March/April 2008 BookSurge controversy:

As we went to press, Amazon.com, the parent of BookSurge, announced that they would require paperback print-on-demand books to be printed by Book-Surge or its sister company, CreateSpace—if they wanted to sell directly on Amazon.com. The company stated that this was to guarantee quick turnaround from the time of order to delivery to the customer. They offered other less attractive alternatives by which authors could sell their books on Amazon.com through resellers or with the Advantage program. And they did not require exclusivity.

We, like many authors and small publishers, are skeptical of the Amazon.com rationale and are concerned about the potential negative impact on price competitiveness. But we accept this as a corporate decision imposed on their subsidiary. That decision doesn't impact the quality of BookSurge's content marketing programs conducted for its authors and itself.

We should also note that BookSurge in March 2008 increased its author royalty from 25% to 35% of the list price of a book sold on Amazon.com. This makes BookSurge a more attractive POD alternative than before.

Chapter Twelve:
Solopreneur Sagas—Even Micro-Businesses Make Content Marketing Pay Off

Three very different small business people are delivering content just as creatively—perhaps more creatively—than many of their peers in much larger organizations.

Type of Organization: Single-person businesses.

Major Marketing Objectives: To use content marketing to increase visibility, credibility, and revenues.

Content Types:

» Websites

» Blogs

» In-person content marketing

Unique Element: Content marketing has replaced traditional marketing for each business.

Results: Each business received a tangible return on its marketing investment.

An author, a kitchen designer, and a seller of smoothies are all making the most of limited budgets to increase revenues and grow their businesses.

Although they're using a diverse combination of online and in-person techniques, they share one common thread: Each entrepreneur is providing content that makes it easier for their target audience to make a positive buying decision. In each case, they are substituting big doses of creativity for big budgets.

Canadian Single Mom May Beat the Odds to Become the Next J.K. Rowling

Multi-pronged content marketing strategy—online and in-person—is helping this self-published author sell books.

Creating a successful business book is difficult. Creating a best-selling work of fiction is even more challenging. Creating a blockbuster children's fantasy novel is probably most difficult of all.

But, thanks to equal doses of determination, creativity, and showmanship, Kamilla Reid of Edmonton, Alberta, is starting to sell a lot of books.

Her fantasy novel, *The Questory of Root Karbunkulus*, is the first in a series of six. It involves the ultimate scavenger hunt by 14-year-old Root, whose very life may be at stake in the adventure. The mystical quest involves a cast of fantastical characters, beasts, and perilous situations.

Kamilla's eclectic background ranges from banking to theater, and now to the writing of children's fiction. For the first time in her life, Kamilla believes that she's doing exactly the right thing. Although she's up against some very steep odds, the early results of her content marketing efforts look very promising indeed.

Kamilla is working with BookSurge (see Chapter Eleven), which is owned by Amazon.com, to produce the book. In fact, BookSurge featured Kamilla in its November 2007 eNewsletter.

Going Way Beyond Amazon.com

The BookSurge connection gives the *Questory* an automatic place within Amazon.com and makes it eligible for all of Amazon's special merchandising and marketing opportunities. Perhaps more importantly for Kamilla, Amazon will also sell volume quantities of its books to its authors at a very low price. This is perfect for Kamilla because it gives her complete freedom to sell and market the book in any way that she chooses. In fact, she is going way beyond what a traditional author would do to promote a book. She is also going way beyond Amazon.com.

Doing What Ernest Hemingway Couldn't or Wouldn't Have Done

With a small budget, you can't hope to replicate the efforts that the publishers of Harry Potter gave their blockbuster hit. However, as Kamilla has proven, you can make things happen with a big dollop of creativity and intelligent use of all the tools available on the web. Her highly imaginative in-person and online content marketing has already taken her well beyond the ranks of typical first-time novelists. She has begun to build a buzz for her book by thinking way outside the binding. Here are some of the innovative things she's doing that may very well take her from Edmonton to New York City and beyond.

Create a miniature play rather than a traditional book signing

Kamilla did not sit demurely behind a desk ready to sign books for parents and children. Rather, she invented a mini-fantasy drama with all kinds of mystical things going on.

She wore a special red cloak that plays a big role in the book. She had magic. She had a big creepy statue. She had mystical mist. It was only after setting the stage brilliantly that she did a wonderfully dramatic reading from the book. The kids lucky enough to have been there absolutely loved it. Best of all, Kamilla sold a lot of books.

*Great videos that make the book, the author,
and the youthful readers very real indeed*

Various types of videos are a major component of the *Questory* website (RootKarbunkulus.com). Here's what you'll find:

» A fun video of the book launch event that fully conveys the excitement of the kids who had the good fortune to be part of the event.

» An exciting video book trailer that does a great job of capturing the spirit of this fantastical novel. You wouldn't know it, but Kamilla shot the video in her basement. And for those of you who know the story of Baby Einstein, that's exactly the way they started—on a bare-bones budget with the first video shot in the basement.

» Video captures of television interviews that show Kamilla dressed in the famous red cloak talking about the book, sharing her enthusiasm, and building awareness among thousands of TV watchers in her home province.

A website that perfectly captures the essence of the book

The look and feel of the site itself is absolutely wonderful. It conveys a sense of drama and mystery, and hints of the secret world we won't know about until we start reading the book. It's exactly the kind of mysterious world that will draw kids in for the first novel—and probably for the next five as well. The *Questory* world looks just scary enough to intrigue kids, but not so frightening as to put them off. In addition to the look of the site, there is an accompanying audio track that reinforces the element of mystery and drama.

The website contains everything you need to know

You can find complete reference information on the website about all things *Questory*:

» A sample chapter

» The complete storyline

» A complete list of the characters (both human and non-human)

» All the new words you'll need to learn to understand the book

» A fascinating bio of Kamilla, complete with pictures

» A press section—entitled buzz that shows all the great coverage she's gotten

» Plus—a store where you can buy the book

Over 1,000 books sold in just seven weeks

Kamilla Reid is selling books, making money, building a buzz, and establishing a foundation that will make it possible to achieve bestseller status. In fact, her creative content marketing efforts generated 1,000 book sales in just seven weeks. That's more than most first-time authors ever sell in a lifetime.

Is it certain that she will accomplish her bestseller ambitions? No. But we certainly wouldn't bet against her.

Kitchen Design Expert's Three-Pronged Web Strategy

Solopreneur takes word-of-mouth to the web.

In many ways Ann Porter, the owner of Kitchen Studio of Naples, is a traditional solopreneur. At the same time, she is also a compelling and creative content marketer. Ann manages to maintain three separate online channels that connect her to current and future customers.

As a traditional solo practitioner, she is an indefatigable networker who relies very much on word-of-mouth to promote her kitchen design business. She belongs to a number of professional and community organizations that connect her to business and consumer prospects. In other words, she does all the things that smart small business people must do to succeed by connecting one-on-one.

Like many small business people, she has found that other forms of traditional marketing have been ineffective in building her business. For example, she advertised with the major lifestyle magazines in the greater Naples area but saw very little return on her substantial investment. She also advertised in the Yellow Pages but found that the caliber of response did not balance the cost of advertising. So…she has taken it to the web.

An Integrated Approach

Ann's three-pronged online strategy includes a standard, well-designed website, her own blog, and a blog she writes on the *Naples Daily News* website. In each case, she does a great job with text and graphics, clearly explaining what she can accomplish for her clients.

An elegant website reflects Ann's design sense

Ann launched her website, KitchenStudioOfNaples.com, in 2002—since then, it has remained virtually unchanged. It is visually appealing and reflects her strong aesthetic sense. It shows her sense of style and the type of kitchen she would design. Like many small business owners, she hired a talented but transitory web developer who no longer lives in the area. What's even more challenging is that the website was built using Flash, which makes for great visuals but which normal human beings cannot manage. So she has begun to rethink the website in terms of a non-Flash design. She knows that optimizing search engine marketing results will be a future priority.

A timely, interactive blog with great design tips and examples

Ann recently launched her blog, KitchAnn Style, using the content management system inside WordPress, which has gone well beyond its blogging roots to become a complete website creation tool. Ann has done 100% of the work herself. Her version of WordPress is absolutely free. Her blog requires time and thought, but no money.

Ann's blog has a clean, sleek look. It's well-organized by category, top posts, and links to external design resources. She uses excellent-quality visuals to illustrate the points she makes about kitchen design issues. Both current and prospective customers will find her blog useful and informative.

In a recent post, Ann illustrated the use of glass panels in the kitchen with the example of a gorgeous contemporary Stuttgart apartment. Because the visual makes the point so well, she didn't need a lot of explanatory text.

Traffic to Ann's blog has been increasing steadily. In fact, it is significantly expanding the word-of-mouth that has been so much a part of her in-person marketing strategy. Ann relates the story of a builder she recently met. He had actually visited her blog before she had time to follow-up on that first meeting. Not surprisingly, he was impressed. Her substantive and well-designed blog gave her instant credibility with the builder after just one meeting.

Pioneers in the User-Generated Content Revolution

The *Naples Daily News*, like many newspapers around the country, is experimenting with user-contributed editorial. One of its most fruitful experiments has been its user-generated blog section. Ann was an early contributor to the section with her Ask Ann weekly blog post.

According to *Naples Daily News* statistics, its weekly reach, both in print and online, is 215,460. Its average household income is $87,482. More than 80% of its readers own their own homes. That's an ideal target audience against which to build a personal and professional brand.

Ann is beginning to receive slow but steady increases in referral traffic as visitors go directly from the *Naples Daily News* to her blog. This is a perfect example of creative content marketing, and, in this case, article marketing. She offers solid kitchen and home design advice to *Naples Daily News* readers with a fresh post each week. She reaches an affluent audience through a trusted newspaper without having to advertise or count on the newspaper to pick up her press releases.

Multiple Avenues Pay Off

Ann Porter has maximized a limited budget, done a lot of hard work, exhibited plenty of creativity, and has developed a consistent approach in order to establish a steadily improving content marketing strategy. The net effect: She has global reach, instant credibility, and a 24/7 sales presence. Word-of-mouth marketing is essential. Taking word-of-mouth to the web is making a measurable difference for Kitchen Studio of Naples.

Simple Visual Blog Delivers Dollars for Maui Wowi Franchisee

Small can be beautiful and profitable when it comes to content marketing.

Although he comes from a sophisticated billion-dollar media company background, Mitch York has left that complex baggage behind. On the web, he keeps it simple. In fact, he delivers just the right amount of information—most of it visual—on his website CoffeesAndSmoothies.com.

Mitch learned from experience that two key factors were making it more difficult than necessary to sell his smoothie services:

» Prospects weren't exactly sure what his company did

» Prospects didn't feel comfortable working with an organization they didn't know or trust

His blog has solved those problems. He now has credibility and his offerings are easy to understand. He has gotten content marketing exactly right and for the right price—free!

When prospects arrive at Mitch's blog (CoffeesAndSmoothies.blogspot. com), they find pictures of happy customers enjoying their smoothies, coffee concoctions, or hot chocolate in a festive environment. Simple captions show the names of customers such as St. Johns University, City College of New York, Bailey Arboretum, and the Fashion Institute of Technology, along with tidbits about the events. The visuals not only make it clear that Mitch is for real, but that his customers have a lot of fun while enjoying his smoothie socials.

On the right side of the blog, Mitch describes exactly what his company does and how to get in touch with him.

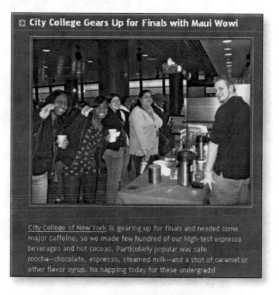

You don't have to be huge to be a big hit

Mitch's website looks great. It tells us exactly what we need to know about what Mitch does and why we can trust him to do it. Wouldn't it be great if some big-time marketers understood content marketing as well as Mitch York?

Mitch built his blog for free using Google's Blogger. He proves that content marketing can be simple, visual, effective, and free. Check out his site—and, if you live in the New York City area, you may want to hire his company to liven up your workplace with a tropical event!

Content Marketing Takeaways

Kamilla, Ann, and Mitch demonstrate the importance of effective content marketing for even very small businesses. For each of them, content marketing plays a vital role because they don't have a sales force or a marketing department or a big budget for traditional advertising.

These creative solopreneurs demonstrate that you can establish credibility with your target audience through effective content marketing strategies. Because their situations are so different, the type of content they provide is also very different:

> » Children's author Kamilla Reid is creating an online and in-person fantasy world in which her prospective readers can immerse themselves.

> » Ann Porter needs to build the perception that she is an established expert in her field with the ability to deliver on sophisticated and expensive kitchen projects.

> » Mitch York must paint an online picture of the types of events he delivers by promoting actual events that prove his company is for real.

For each of them, the initial content marketing investment was relatively modest. Better yet, their ongoing investment is very, very low. They need to keep putting in the time—but not additional marketing dollars—to make their content marketing strategies pay off. ❖

Chapter Thirteen:
Content Marketing Pays Off on the Bottom Line in Australia

How Bitemark teaches small- and medium-sized businesses to reinvent their online presence to deliver dramatic increases in sales, leads, and profits.

Type of Organization: Website and eNewsletter developer in Melbourne, Australia.

Major Marketing Objective: To attract new clients with its website, blog, and eNewsletter.

Content Types:

» Website

» Blog

» eNewsletter

Unique Element: Unlike many web developers, Bitemark has done an in-depth study of what types of content and design will produce tangible sales results for clients.

Results: Online content marketing works for Bitemark because most of its growth comes from clients who have discovered them online.

"We are really thinking like publishers," says Brett Gilbertson, Bitemark's director of marketing. In terms of content marketing, "it's been a complete mind shift." This applies equally to websites, blogs, and eNewsletters. Brad and his team are recognized today as online marketing experts Down Under. They would be just as effective if they were headquartered in San Francisco or New York City.

Bitemark didn't start out to teach its Australian customers how to create websites that prompted action, leads, and sales. But it wound up filling a void it didn't know existed.

Bitemark first offered software solutions that enabled web professionals to build sophisticated websites. But technology wasn't the answer to creating results-driven websites.

Today, Bitemark provides a full-range of online services that enable its clients to transform old-fashioned, brochure-ware sites into content-rich websites, and eNewsletters that turn visitors into buyers.

For Brett and his clients, it's all about driving measurable results. Bitemark has studied what works and what doesn't. It is continually fine-tuning its efforts to be certain it drives sales and profits on behalf of its clients.

Bitemark's content creation expertise evolved only after it realized that web developers did not understand the need for relevant content. Nor did the developers' clients. Bitemark also realized that the vast majority of businesses were clueless about creating websites that produced leads and sales.

Brett estimates that fewer than 10% of small- to medium-sized businesses understand the importance of content marketing. "Great content isn't just about making prospects smarter and better informed," he says. "Great content is really about delivering sales and marketing results."

Brett reiterates this idea on his blog. His company makes its living by building websites. But not just ordinary websites. Although its websites look great and typically have strong visuals combined with clear intuitive navigation, that's not the point. The company's objective is simple: it builds sites for clients that generate plenty of leads and plenty of sales. It does this through results-oriented content marketing.

Brett stresses:

> *"Effectively dealing with the infinite choices consumers have on the web involves a mind shift from old marketing where commercial messages are thrust on people. The messages that work best on the web are those that consumers choose. There's a huge benefit to making this mind shift—it then becomes easy to create the kind of content that your customers are looking for."*

In other words, make sure that your content is customer-centric.

Brett's team is very clear about why most websites get it all wrong. They don't pull any punches on their website, when they say:

> *"Unfortunately, most of the time…businesses do this with their websites:*

» Talk about themselves more than their customers

» Use jargon that their customers don't understand

» Make it difficult for their customers to find them

» Distract them with unnecessary sizzle and clutter

» Hide behind their websites by not giving out contact details

» Leave their customers wondering what to do next

» The list goes on...

"It's not confidence-inspiring. The upside for you is that it's not hard to stand out with your web marketing."

Brett emphasizes that the ideal solution integrates a solution-oriented website, effective search engine optimization, and a blog. "This is a very powerful combination," he says.

Brett adds that it's essential to understand what problems your target customers are trying to solve—and then to make it obvious on your website that your company is ready, willing, and able to solve those problems.

Leading by Content Marketing Example

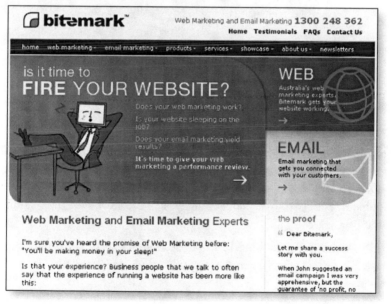

The Bitemark website immediately grabs your attention with a strong visual—and an equally strong challenge question: *"Is it time to fire your website?"*

One of the website's strengths is that it doesn't waste words. With typical Aussie directness, it gets right down to business, using lots of brief sentences in bullet points accompanied by relevant graphics. The Bitemark site is also full of case studies, examples, and testimonials.

Bitemark also makes it clear that you can expect a certain level of service and performance from them. If they fail to perform, Bitemark expects you to call them on it.

You come away trusting that they know what they're doing, that you can benefit from their help, and that you can count on them to do the job.

Bitemark's Conversion Rate Blog: Guaranteed to Make You a Better Content Marketer

Brett himself writes the popular Conversion Rate blog, which typically tackles complex online marketing issues. Recently, he provided an in-depth examination of good and bad e-mail marketing practices. Regular readers of the blog benefit from his cogent analysis, which is based on a significant amount of research.

While examining e-mail marketing issues, he put together a rogue's gallery of terrible preview pane examples, as well as winner's circle of great e-mail examples.

In another recent blog series, he evaluated how it might still be possible to use the online Yellow Pages for affordable lead generation. He determined that if you invest in the top level of advertising and make sure that your ad content is solution-focused (rather than being all about your company), you can expect to generate a solid return on your advertising investment. Even though he talked about advertising rather than content marketing in this case, it still goes back to being customer-centric in your messaging.

Brett's blog is valuable because it provides thoughtful content that deals with universal problems that online marketers face when they try to generate tangible results from their efforts.

As with all great blogs, by providing real benefit to its readers, Conversion Rate provides just as much benefit to Bitemark.

Delivering Tangible Results for Customers with Limited Marketing Budgets

Bitemark's single-minded focus on content, which assures visitors that it can provide solutions, is delivering measurable results for clients such as Fort Knox Self Storage and Ace Mobile Mechanics. Both of these clients were struggling with typical first-generation websites that offered little incentive for visitors to move toward a purchase.

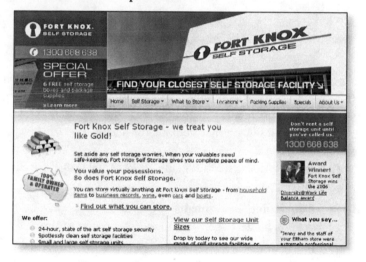

Fort Knox Self Storage now has a visually appealing, action-oriented site that makes it obvious why you would want to store your possessions with them. It has increased the number of leads substantially, with an impressive 4%-5% conversion rate.

Ace Mobile Mechanics' website presented it as "the cheapest in town," and didn't even provide a phone number. At the time, the company's primary source of leads was the Yellow Pages, where it was spending $100,000 per year. Ace invested $10,000 with Bitemark for a 10-page website that is delivering an astonishing 19% conversion rate. Ace's web presence is now its lowest-cost source of leads. In 2008, the website will edge out the Yellow Pages in the total number of leads.

Relatively small online investments are producing dramatic results for Bitemark's clients. Its biggest challenge—and perhaps yours as well—is convincing traditional marketers to change the way they think about marketing. Those efforts have not been easy, but have been well worth the effort based on the bottom-line results that Bitemark's clients are achieving.

Content Marketing Takeaways

Thinking like a publisher is fundamental to developing and executing a successful content marketing strategy. As we explained in Chapter Three, thinking like a publisher means figuring out what information is essential to your customers and then delivering it in a compelling way. Typically, this means helping them solve a problem or giving them ways to live a more successful professional or personal life.

When it comes to great websites, pure good looks and spiffy technology are meaningless if they don't reinforce relevant content.

If you are in any kind of marketing business, you must provide persuasive examples of content marketing that prove you can actually generate results for your customers. Your website should be your single best source of qualified leads and sales, as traditional marketing avenues diminish in value.

If you're writing a business blog, bring benefit to your customers first. Then benefits will naturally flow to you. ❖

Chapter Fourteen:
You Can Trust Northern Trust to Deploy a Great Content Marketing Strategy

Northern's implementation mirrors the excellence of its customer care and understanding.

Type of Organization: Global bank catering to wealthy clients with $63.1 billion in banking assets.

Major Marketing Objective: To use print and online content to reinforce its "wealth" thought leadership with its very wealthy clients and important third-party wealth advisors.

Content Types:

> » Print magazine for clients

> » Website for clients

> » Microsite for wealth advisors

> » eNewsletter for wealth advisors

Unique Element: Targeted content for outside advisors who influence current and future Northern Trust clients.

Results: Client-centered content combined with impeccable execution of its financial services has helped Northern Trust maintain a dominant market position as the private bank that even its competitors concede is the best in the business.

The Northern Trust folks have always been good marketers—particularly when it came to in-person events and community involvement. For example, each year they bring in their top investment professionals to present their best investment advice to capacity client crowds. They also provide custom events for the wealth advisors who look after their clients.

Northern Trust's people-to-people focus accurately reflects the way it cares for its clients—and the in-depth knowledge that its people are willing and able to convey. But it's not all about the money. In fact, each year the company hosts hundreds of clients on wonderfully unique vacation trips all over the world. Sometimes, a client's just got to have fun.

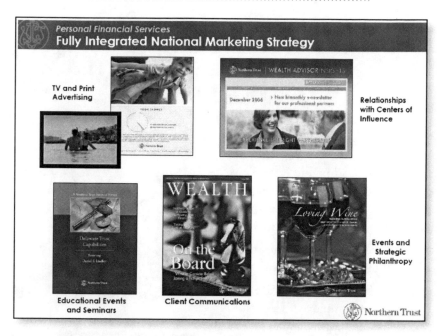

Applying Client Understanding to a Content Marketing Strategy

Recently, Northern Trust began to extend the reach and quality of its content to print and online products. In fact, in their presentations to financial analysts, Northern Trust representatives discuss their fully integrated marketing program, as the accompanying graphic shows. This people-to-people implementation of content marketing reinforces already strong relationships.

Northern Trust is very clear on its mission, which is to *"provide comprehensive, customized, and innovative financial solutions for successful individuals, families, and their businesses."*

Three outstanding content marketing implementations illustrate Northern Trust's clear understanding of what is truly important to its clients:

» A content-rich, beautifully designed quarterly magazine entitled *Wealth*

» A client website that is much more client-centric today than it was just two years ago

» Interrelated content products that target expert independent wealth advisors who serve Northern Trust clients

Wealth: **Sophisticated Advice for Northern Trust Clients**

Creating a magazine that genuinely reflects the passions and interests of its affluent clientele came naturally, because Northern Trust understands its clients so well. *Wealth* is beautifully designed on high-quality, heavy paper stock. The articles are substantial, precisely targeted, and highly informative. Because there is no advertising, the amount of content delivered is equal to that of a magazine twice its size.

Here are some things its affluent readers learned in the Fall 2007 issue:

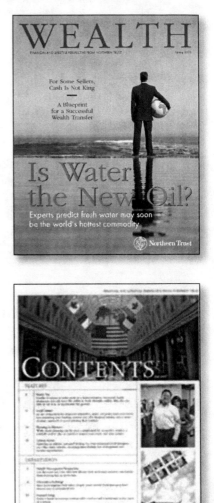

» How to adopt the kind of best practices employed by institutional investors when it comes to managing a substantial portfolio

» How to employ a risk-management strategy when a high percentage of your portfolio isn't a single stock—as part of a company sale for example

» How to work through conflict so that a family business can achieve longevity

» How one "serial social entrepreneur" uses a for-profit model to achieve non-profit goals—and thus achieve long-term financial stability

» And a bit of fun stuff, such as an article about whole-house automation

In this issue of the magazine, there are only two brief items—totaling just half a page—that talk about Northern Trust news. Everything else is completely customer-centric.

The implicit message that Northern delivers? "We care about your well-being and have the knowledge and resources to protect it."

A Client-Centric Website

Northern Trust's client-centric website is visually appealing, well-organized, and chock-full of content. It is better in several important ways from its predecessor of just a few years ago. The old site:

» Began with a very long description of Northern Trust, which was all about Northern Trust, not the client

» Had a very small visual element

» Didn't really give the appearance of being client-centric

» Required a fair amount of work to access information

» Had a lot of information, but included many disparate elements that lacked an easy-to-follow structure

The new website—both client-centric and client-friendly—is better in every way. It gives the impression of a bank you can trust and enjoy doing business with. The new site:

» Leads with a wonderfully warm visual of a father swinging his young daughter on a sunny day; to the right of the photo is a graphic titled "having your cake and eating it too," which illustrates the balance between having a good quarter and having a good life.

» Has a very simple, three-column division between personal services, institutional services, and the "About Northern Trust" section.

» Features a "Knowledge Center" that gives clients access to an incredible amount of financial and economic information—all of which is logically organized.

» Offers podcasts of weekly discussions by Northern Trust experts on topics such as unique approaches to institutional investing, global pension plans, and timely tax tips.

What about that long description about Northern Trust that used to appear so prominently? It's still on the site, but instead of being in giant green letters at the top, it now appears in small black type at the bottom.

Northern Trust Delivers Targeted Content to Wealth Advisors

Northern Trust understands that if advisors don't understand its culture and mission, there is no way they'll be able to convey it to end-customers. That's why advisor communication is one of the most important aspects of the Northern Trust integrated marketing plan.

Northern Trust's visually appealing microsite, NorthernTrust.com/wealthadvisor, was designed specifically for this audience. Here, they can find:

» Detailed information on client solutions

» A broad range of in-depth information relating to financial and wealth services

» Podcasts they can listen to at their convenience

» A series of white papers that offer content to help advisors deal with specific client needs

» Access to *Wealth* magazine in PDF or HTML format, which also includes hyperlinks to even more resources

Northern Trust also produces a bimonthly eNewsletter that provides up-to-date information on many of the complex issues that wealth advisors must understand in order to best advise their affluent clients. This eNewsletter, in turn, reminds them to connect back to the dedicated microsite.

Content Marketing Takeaways

Northern Trust has always had an in-depth understanding of its wealthy clients, which has enabled the organization to shape a culture of trust that has inspired long-term client relationships. This understanding made the development of a comprehensive content marketing strategy a natural extension of the way it cares for its clients. Without it, Northern Trust would have failed to create relevant and valuable content.

Additionally, Northern Trust has always excelled at providing in-person content for its clients in small- and large-group settings. The information it provides has a single objective: to make clients smarter and better informed about managing substantial individual, family, and business assets. This tradition of in-person content marketing was the natural precursor to print and online products.

Providing valuable content for third-party advisors positions Northern Trust as a trusted partner. By delivering focused content—with no expectation of immediate return—that enables these advisors to better serve wealthy clients, Northern Trust becomes the logical source for a broad range of financial services. ❖

Chapter Fifteen:
Leveraging Content Marketing to Strengthen Member and Community Relationships

The Greater Naples Chamber of Commerce improved its publications and, in turn, increased revenue.

Type of Organization: Chamber of Commerce with nearly 2,000 members.

Major Marketing Objective: To improve the quality of its publications to maximize member benefits and increase chamber revenues.

Content Types:

» Monthly magazine

» Website

» eNewsletter

Unique Element: The chamber manages the content of its publications internally, thus improving quality while reducing cost and growing revenues.

Results: Revenue and membership growth, both of which can be attributed directly to content-driven products that provide value to members and the community.

All associations and chambers of commerce succeed based on their ability to deliver measurable value to their members. But many of their efforts are intangible and therefore hard to measure. As a result, members often wonder whether they're getting their money's worth.

One of the best ways to transform the intangible benefits that a membership organization provides is to create information products that communicate effectively with members—and with targeted members of the business community in which the organization operates.

Although it's relatively easy to generate printed or online publications, it's much more difficult to make them relevant and compelling. That was a challenge that the Greater Naples Chamber of Commerce faced in the spring of 2006. In addition, as with most membership organizations, generating non-dues-related income is essential to the viability of the organization. That means that sponsorships and advertising can make a significant difference. So, too, can high-quality events and publications.

The Naples Business Community: Lots of Very Small Companies

Although the greater Naples business community comprises a number of very large companies, the vast majority of local businesses have fewer than 25 employees. Chamber membership reflects this reality. Large organizations may join a chamber because it's the right thing to do or because they believe they must be involved with the larger business community. Smaller companies with very limited budgets take a much more pragmatic view of things.

Although small-company dues may be less than $300 per year, that's a significant expenditure for most. Therefore, these companies want to know that they are getting measurable value from their investment. If the owners participate actively in chamber events and on chamber committees, they will probably feel that they get full value from the connections they make month after month.

However, many owners spend most of their time focusing on their business operations and may have little time left over to allocate to chamber events or other business-related organizations.

In order to retain these busy business owners as members, keeping them at least virtually engaged with the chamber is all-important. This boils down to regularly providing them with content that matches their most important information needs. If this content is delivered in a format that permits members to advertise affordably, so much the better.

In addition to its website, the Greater Naples Chamber of Commerce offers *Business Currents*, a monthly business magazine, and *Leadership Link*, a monthly eNewsletter.

Providing Vital Content Creates Tangible Value for Members

In 2006, the Greater Naples Chamber of Commerce was making a significant monthly investment in multiple publications. But it was uncertain if these content marketing efforts were truly serving member information needs. In addition, it had to add or improve non-dues-related revenue in order to fund its many business, community, and public policy initiatives.

One of its first undertakings was to transform chamber publications from "good" to "great." The Naples chamber has always been deeply committed to providing essential information to its members, but, like most smaller chambers, it had never had staff members with extensive publishing experience who could create truly great publications.

Its monthly newsprint-style publication always had a number of good articles, but there was no consistent editorial structure to the publication. Nor was there an annual editorial calendar to give it focus and consistency. Moreover, the chamber was outsourcing much of the work of producing its print newsletter, which was fine, but the integration of customer needs and vendor support was disjointed.

In addition to the monthly publication, the chamber maintained a website that served as a central point for its membership directory and for event management. In theory, it was also an outlet for current news. But because it was so difficult to manage (no simple content management system), keeping the website current was almost impossible.

Let's take a look at how the chamber became more content marketing-oriented.

Step One: Understand the Business Information that Is Most Important to Your Members.

As of Spring 2006, the chamber had not done a recent study among its members to determine what topics and issues were most important to them. This made it quite difficult to provide relevant content on any kind of consistent basis.

Therefore, the first step in the transformation of the chamber publications was to figure out what members really wanted to know. This was part of a broader effort to make the chamber more customer-centric.

The chamber surveyed its members to determine:

» What they thought about the content the chamber was currently providing

» How relevant they found that content, in terms of their information needs

» What types of articles they preferred

» What business-related issues they most wanted to receive information on

» How they rated the design of the current publication

They learned that the newsletter, *Currents*, was well-read. That was the good news. The bad news was that it was not highly rated in terms of relevance to the members' information needs. The study also uncovered exactly what types of information members would really find relevant. This provided the data needed to reinvent the newsletter so that it would become a "must-read" publication.

The chamber took the production of its monthly publication in-house because it finally had the staff resources and expertise to create a great new monthly magazine. Catherine Dentino, the new communications manager, was a talented writer and editor as well as an outstanding graphic designer.

Step Two: Translate Research into a Publication that Is Genuinely Relevant to Business Owners and Executives.

The chamber team was able to translate the research findings into the beginnings of a high-quality monthly magazine. The key elements were as follows:

- » Research indicated that a glossy 8.5" x 11" magazine with full-color throughout would significantly increase the perception of quality.

- » Chamber members had given extensive rankings to the topics and issues most important to them. This enabled the team to create an editorial calendar that was a real roadmap to significantly enhanced editorial content.

- » A design prototype was created so that key decision makers, including the chamber CEO, Mike Reagan, and members of the board of directors could give constructive feedback.

- » The publication was renamed *Business Currents* to more accurately reflect its core business focus.

- » A media kit was created, which focused on the "research-driven" nature of the improved publication.

- » A low-cost, high-quality offset printing company was selected to produce the magazine each month.

- » It was determined that chamber staff would be able to edit and design the publication each month.

- » Respected business leaders and subject matter experts would also contribute content regularly on a voluntary basis.

- » A detailed production schedule was created so that the magazine would come out on-time each and every month.

- » The chamber's sales staff was trained in how to sell advertising to appear in the new publication.

Although the initial level of effort required to bring the magazine in-house was daunting, the chamber was able to produce a high-quality monthly magazine that premiered in October 2006. By instituting detailed editorial processes and schedules, the chamber has been able to consistently deliver a high-quality publication.

As a bonus, the new and improved magazine was less expensive to produce—plus it generated significantly more advertising revenue in support of chamber activities.

More than one year later, *Business Currents* continues to thrive, tackling tough business and community issues that significantly impact chamber members. Despite staffing changes, the chamber continues to maintain quality of both design and content.

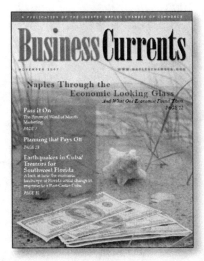

Unlike many chamber and association publications, *Business Currents* doesn't gloss over significant challenges that face the business community.

In the November 2007 issue, for example, it included a stark but objective assessment of the local economy. Another hard-hitting article explored the implications of a reopening of Cuba, which poses a serious threat to the vital tourism segment of Southwest Florida.

Although *Business Currents* also does a great job of covering chamber events, the real heart of the publication is its solid coverage of business, public policy, and community issues. In addition, it's chock-full of practical advice on how to run your business better.

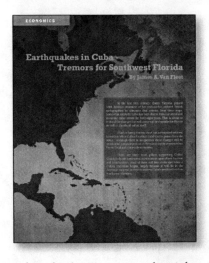

This critical mass of compelling content generates excellent readership. Readership, in turn, is what makes advertising effective. Because advertisers know that they're getting to the right business buyers in a publication that is valued by those buyers, they know they're in the right magazine.

Business Currents' quality content is significantly enhanced by its excellent design—which is led-off by memorable covers that motivate business executives to pick up the magazine the moment it lands on their desks.

Step Three: Create an Invaluable Website for Members, Business Owners, and Visitors.

The chamber's next major content task was to upgrade its website, Naples Chamber.org, which was built on antiquated technology, was hard to manage, and offered good but limited content.

The biggest challenge in creating a great chamber website is that it must serve multiple constituencies: chamber members, prospective members, business owners and executives, tourists, and visitors. Moreover, although much of the content is relatively timeless, a significant portion of it must be kept current. In addition, because it is an event hub, it must provide e-commerce capabilities.

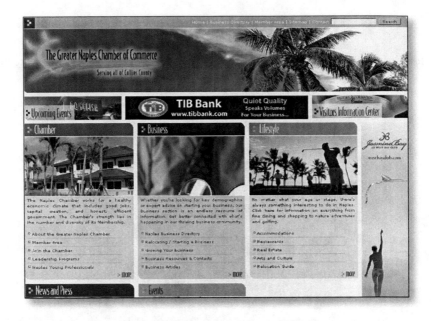

The chamber partnered with a Naples-based advertising and web design firm, ISOOSI, that fully understands the importance of first-rate content and a user-friendly interface. ISOOSI is unusual in that its understanding of content marketing is just as strong as its ability to design great websites.

To provide robust transactional capabilities, the chamber also licensed web-based software technology from WebLink. This provides excellent back-end capabilities that integrate with the chamber's accounting system, providing an easy-to-use management system. In addition, it provides all the e-commerce tools required to manage dozens of yearly events. Very importantly, the website is easy and inexpensive to maintain by chamber staffers.

Today, NaplesChamber.org draws a broad range of traffic. After the redesign, web traffic increased dramatically as members, residents, and tourists accessed much-improved content more frequently. In September 2007, there were 45,729 visitors—that's an increase of more than 600% from September 2006.

The redesigned website has a simple and intuitive design that makes it obvious when you reach the homepage exactly where you should go for the type of information that you need. In addition, the website is now the go-to spot to learn about and register for chamber events. This makes it much easier to manage events in order to provide even more events that benefit the members.

The chamber continues to work closely with ISOOSI to maintain and improve NaplesChamber.org. The website has a great deal of invaluable content that includes:

> » What you need to know if you're planning to relocate a business to Southwest Florida
>
> » How to start a business locally
>
> » How to run your business more effectively
>
> » A comprehensive business directory with e-mail and mapping capability
>
> » Information about chamber business education events
>
> » Information about chamber networking events
>
> » The ability to sign-up and pay for chamber events online
>
> » Comprehensive tourist and visitor information
>
> » Comprehensive relocation information
>
> » And on and on and on…

In short, NaplesChamber.org not only provides a treasure trove of information for its current and prospective members, it also serves as an extraordinary resource for the community.

Step Four: Retool Monthly eNewsletter to Address Both Business and Community Concerns.

In 2007, the chamber significantly improved the quality of its eNewsletter, *Leadership Link*. Its monthly content includes coverage of both community and business topics—particularly focusing on the importance of leadership skills.

The December 2007 issue featured:

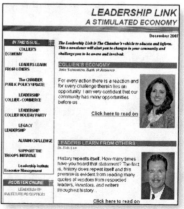

> » A commentary on current economic challenges in Southwest Florida by a Bank of America vice president who is also the new head of the local Economic Development Council
>
> » An article on leadership by a former city executive who is currently a professor at Florida State University

» A public policy update from a senior business executive who is on the chamber's board of directors

» Articles on Collier County leadership programs

» Links to a variety of business and community resources

Again, the chamber is reaching out to the Naples community with content that is relevant to the most pressing issues of the day. It reinforces the chamber's leadership role in the community—and reminds its members how much value they are receiving from their membership. Finally, it performs the practical role of linking readers back to the NaplesChamber.org website so that they're reminded each month of how much relevant business content the chamber is delivering.

The chamber's content marketing efforts help both the chamber and its members succeed. Although the chamber cannot specifically attribute membership strength to its much-improved content, its membership continues to grow, despite a weak local and national economy.

Content Marketing Takeaways

Although the chamber has nearly 2,000 members, it is a small organization with limited resources. But it has learned that by providing a rich variety of meaningful content to its members and to the broader community, it can extend its reach and impact dramatically. What it cannot do in-person, it can achieve in print and online via *Business Currents*, NaplesChamber.org, and *Leadership Link*.

Through its content marketing efforts, the chamber goes a long way toward making the intangible benefits of membership much more tangible. Thus, when busy entrepreneurs take the time to read the chamber's materials, the value of their membership becomes very clear indeed.

The chamber's core print and online publications deliver a level of revenue that significantly exceeds that of the older-generation information products. The ability to generate revenue derives directly from the improved product quality. ❖

Chapter Sixteen:
At Best Buy, It's All About Strengthening Customer Relationships

Best Buy is reinventing its entire company around the concept of customer-centricity. It has learned that a deep understanding of its ideal customers results in a host of trusted relationships, which, in turn, drive sales and profits.

Type of Organization: Multi-billion-dollar electronics and appliance retailer.

Major Marketing Objective: To find a way to build strong, lasting relationships with its very best customers.

Content Types:

» Print magazine

» Electronic magazine version

Unique Element: Content discusses products, services, and activities that relate to lifestyle, not to Best Buy.

Results: Trusted relationships with biggest spenders are strengthened via an enthusiast publication that provides no apparent benefit to Best Buy.

While Circuit City was cutting, Best Buy was adding. Why? Because, at its heart, customer-centricity is all about providing excellent customer service.

But customer-centricity is much more than that. It involves determining who your best customers are and how best to serve them. Here is how *Fortune* magazine described the Best Buy vision of customer-centricity in its March 29, 2006, issue:

> *"Figure out which customers make you the most money, segment them carefully, then realign your stores and empower employees to target those favored shoppers with products and services that will encourage them to spend more and come back often."*

Best Buy has gone so far as to create elaborately described personas for its most important customers. One would be Jill, a busy suburban mom. Another would be Barry, an affluent tech enthusiast. An enormous amount of work is involved to prepare individual stores to cater to particular personas. Thus, a "Jill store" would be specially configured to match up with her shopping habits and product interests. It would also have personal shopping assistants who would help her pick out just the right gadgets for her family and show her how to use them.

Best Buy has expanded its service focus dramatically over the last five years. The Geek Squad, which it acquired from a startup in 2005, now numbers more than 17,000 technical support professionals. The ubiquitous geeks represent Best Buy's understanding of the need for high-touch customer care.

In fact, customer-centricity equates to enlightened self-interest that benefits both the customer and Best Buy.

Improving the Experience and Growing Share

Best Buy's continued focus on an ever-improving customer experience closely tracks its significantly increased U.S. market share. In a recent presentation to Morgan Stanley, Best Buy showed that as its computer return and exchange rate had dropped significantly between 2001 and 2006, its market share continued to expand—from roughly 14% in 2001 (pre-Geek Squad) to slightly more than 20% in 2006. Here is how they described it in the Morgan Stanley presentation:

> *"You can trust Best Buy and Geek Squad to make your computer and everything you connect to it always work seamlessly so that you can enjoy your passions. This is why we come to work."*

Best Magazine Exemplifies Content Built on Customer-Centricity

Best Magazine doesn't go to just anybody. Only Best Buy's very best customers receive it. This careful targeting derives from the customer-centricity concept of treating your most profitable customers in a very special way.

Senior Vice President of Marketing Barry Judge explains that *Best Magazine* is designed to "share our passion about how technology can enhance their lives."

As Best Buy's top marketing executive, Judge guides its brand strategy; he drives the development of new marketing capabilities and empowers marketing innovation as the company transforms to put the customer at the center of its business model.

Judge believes that it is essential "to build credibility from a trusted perspective by making it clear that there is no obvious way that Best Buy will benefit" from the creation and distribution of *Best Magazine*.

He adds that the publication has generated a "pleasantly happy customer reaction," and concludes that *Best Magazine* provides value "precisely because it doesn't appear to sell Best Buy."

Best Buy has learned that a deep understanding of its ideal customers results in a host of trusted relationships, which, in turn, drive sales and profits. Building on that understanding, the retailing giant continues to add value to the customer experience because it has learned, as Judge says: "When we invest in our customers, they will invest more heavily with us."

Best Magazine contains absolutely no promotion for Best Buy. Except for a welcoming icon on the cover, the company takes a back seat to the magazine's content.

The magazine itself is an enthusiast's paradise. Loaded with product information about everything from iPods to sports cars, the colorful, 76-page periodical tells readers all about what's "best" and how to get maximum enjoyment from the huge range of products it covers.

In a recent issue, *Best Magazine* profiled an eclectic assortment of sport coupes:

> *"But instead of arguing semantics, we preferred to play free as-sociation with driving enthusiasts. Given the stimulus of the word 'coupe', this passionate demographic responded with 'fast', 'exhilarating', 'sport', and—last but not least—'two-door hard-top'... we simply want to demonstrate that, when you're talk-ing two-door sport coupes, grins come in all sizes and prices."*

Another article, aimed at sports fans who want to emulate professional sports photographers, explains how to get that perfect action shot. Here's the kind of immediately useful advice you get from the author, sports photogra-pher extraordinaire, Peter Read Miller:

> *"In all my years shooting sports for* Sports Illustrated, *I've found no substitute for preparation when on an assignment. If you want to get that perfect shot, you can plan ahead, too... There used to be a great spot at the old Mile High Stadium, in Denver, where there was a gap in the stands. As the sun went down, beautiful golden light would stream through the open space. When players hit the right spot, it created an amaz-ing effect: They would be bathed in light, but the background would be in shadow."*

Best Magazine is a genuine enthusiast publication in the finest tradition of *Sports Illustrated, Car and Driver, Flying,* and *Audiophile.* Although it does cover lots of technical gadgets and electronic paraphernalia, its editorial con-tent ranges far beyond that. Of course, the publication is aimed squarely at Best Buy's frequent, big-ticket buyers who love to acquire the latest and greatest—and to learn how to put those products to work for maximum en-joyment and satisfaction. And that's exactly what *Best Magazine* teaches them to do.

Online *Best Magazine* Gets Even Cooler

The publication adds another layer of cool in its electronic version. It is clearly designed to be read online with scrolling text that makes room for very large and high-impact graphical elements. Rather than a hodgepodge of ban-ner ads that typically confront website visitors, the online magazine ads have all of the colorful impact of those in the print version. Even better, many of its ads go from static to interactive. The example shown here is a live video ad from Sony showing off its high-definition DVD player. All in all, the online version of *Best Magazine* delivers a superior experience.

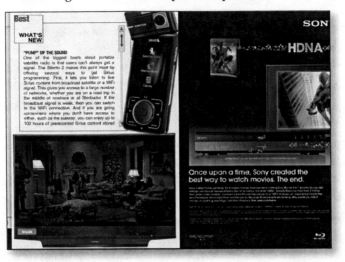

Content Marketing Takeaways

When you really understand your customers and what they need, you're perfectly positioned to provide content that positions you as a trusted provider—first of information, and then of products and services. Best Buy has learned that you must take excellent care of your very best customers. It does this in a number of ways, of which *Best Magazine* is the perfect content example.

Best Buy is reinventing itself around the concept of customer-centricity. This takes customer understanding to a new depth. It means that you must identify both your very best customers and your very worst customers. You need to cherish the very best and perhaps dump the very worst. For those ideal customers, carefully crafting a precisely targeted information product such as *Best Magazine* will enable you to strengthen those all-important customer relationships.

Although Best Buy has a huge marketing budget and can afford to create a 76-page, four-color print magazine, you can accomplish a similar objective less expensively. You can create a more highly focused publication that targets the vital information needs of customers with whom you want to forge long-term partnerships. As they begin to count on you as a reliable source of vital information, you will take a special place in the ranks of their suppliers. ❖

Chapter Seventeen:
Using Content Marketing to Accelerate the
Acceptance of a Concept and a Product

Chapter Seventeen:
Using Content Marketing to Accelerate the Acceptance of a Concept and a Product

Mindjet uses content marketing extensively to grow its sales because word-of-mouth is the single most important factor in the success of its products.

Type of Organization: Privately held software company that sells mind-mapping software worldwide to 1 million users.

Major Marketing Objective: To use online content to extend the understanding and use of its mindmapping software.

Content Types:

> » Website
>
> » eNewsletter
>
> » Blog
>
> » Webcasts

Unique Element: The Mindjet team created a personalized mindmap for a new product launch aimed at reporters and analysts. By giving the reporters and analysts an actual tool they could use in their work and personal lives, the Mindjet team demonstrated why roadmapping (and the product Mind-Manager) is so valuable.

Results: Mindjet has been able to replace all its traditional marketing methods with online content strategy, culminating in its most successful product launch in 2007.

San Francisco-based software company Mindjet has been developing mindmapping software since 1993. Since 2004, it has grown dramatically from three dozen employees to almost 165—and more than 1 million users.

Mindmapping is a different way of thinking from the traditional vertical outline that we all learned in school. It involves a radial model with a core concept at the center and branches and sub-branches extending from that core.

Although it does take a bit of explaining, former Mindjet marketing executive Katy Colletto likens the incredible productivity improvement she experienced when she started using MindManager to the difference between schlepping an old-fashioned suitcase and the ease of strolling along with a suitcase on wheels. As she puts it: "Today I can't imagine how I ever got along without MindManager."

Mindmapping is a wonderful way to improve your thinking, get yourself organized, and enhance your creativity. If you know about mindmapping, you know exactly what I'm talking about. If you don't know about mindmapping, I'll need to do some explaining.

Although in the U.S. we learn to organize our thoughts in linear outlines, mindmapping theory suggests that our minds don't really think that way.

Wikipedia defines a mindmap as:

> "*An image-centered diagram that represents semantic or other connections between portions of information. By presenting these connections in a radial, non-linear graphical manner, it encourages a brainstorming approach to any given organizational task, eliminating the hurdle of initially establishing an intrinsically appropriate or relevant conceptual framework to work within...The elements are arranged intuitively according to the importance of the concepts and they are organized into groupings, branches, or areas.*"

The best way to understand mindmapping is to grab a large piece of paper and some colored pencils and pens—and just begin putting down your thoughts, beginning with the central point.

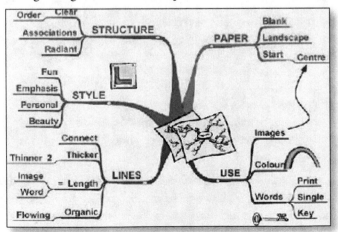

Chapter Seventeen:
Using Content Marketing to Accelerate the
Acceptance of a Concept and a Product

Use single words or very short phrases for each category and related subcategory. Make your map as colorful and as creative as you can. If you're writing down a list of current projects, you'll want to include all the most important elements for each project. If you're even the least bit visual, you will find that even a rudimentary mindmap elicits creative thoughts and ideas that surprise you. And if you're a process person, mindmapping will add structure, efficiency, and creativity to your days.

Recently, the *Wall Street Journal* mentioned MindManager as an effective organizational tool:

> *"Fans say mindmapping software can give them a single view of all the aspects of a project. It gives an 'air-traffic controller view of what you're doing,' says William R. Miller, a controller for the information-technology group at a unit of Nationwide Financial Services Inc."* (*WSJ*, December 11, 2007)

Mindjet's growth parallels the increasing acceptance of the concept of mindmapping. But, in spite of Mindjet's success, it faces a significant marketing challenge: Unless you know what mindmappping is, it is difficult to explain.

That makes traditional advertising relatively ineffective. Even print advertorials did not do the trick for Mindjet. To overcome the disappointing results that it got from print advertising, Mindjet began to pursue a creative online content marketing strategy.

Putting Word-of-Mouth to Work on the Web

Fortunately for Mindjet, it has incredible word-of-mouth; in fact 60% to 80% of its sales are driven by viral marketing. Even better, 85% of its users consider themselves "evangelists."

Therefore, Mindjet's primary efforts involve extending the reach and impact of these evangelists. It has determined that most MindManager users tend to focus on a single application for mindmapping. Mindjet is convinced that by educating these enthusiasts in all the ways that MindManager can improve productivity, process, and creativity, it will grow both the users and the uses of the product.

A Website that Really Works

When you land at Mindjet.com, the first thing you'll probably notice is a headline that explains exactly what Mindjet is all about: *"Work smarter, think creatively, save time…every day Mindjet helps people visualize and use information."*

The Mindjet website presents a wealth of compelling content that revolves around the visual metaphor of a mind map. Mindjet.com is very much a get-to-the-point website that takes you exactly where you want to go. Whether you want to learn about business productivity, examine a powerful case study, review some very cool mind mapping templates built with MindManager, or contact support, you can find everything easily.

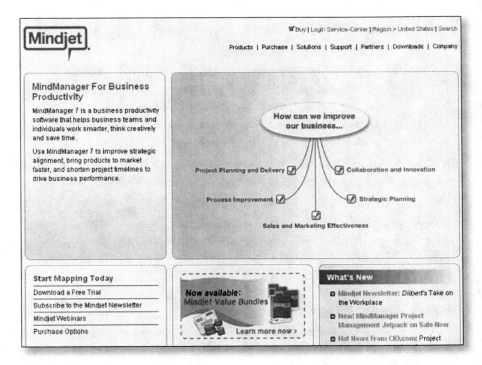

For example, you can link directly to the business productivity page where the major feature is a large MindMap with live links to in-depth business productivity examples. Thus, if you click on a strategic planning link, you go directly to a page that explains simply how MindManager enables strategic planning. There you will find even more links to sample maps, case studies, recorded webinars, and white papers.

Mindjet's website is packed full of content that offers intrinsic value whether or not you ever decide to buy its software. Of course, much of that content is so compelling that you are pretty darn likely to become a new customer after you've read through it. Appropriately, when you're ready to buy the product, the website makes it incredibly easy to do so.

Chapter Seventeen:
Using Content Marketing to Accelerate the
Acceptance of a Concept and a Product

And then There's a Really Useful Monthly eNewsletter

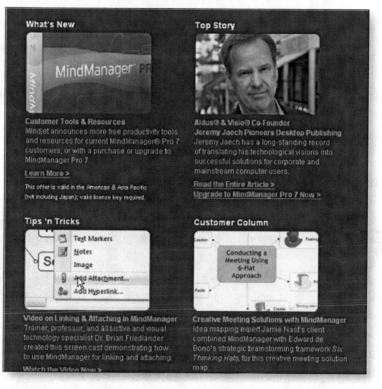

The Mindjet eNewsletter focuses almost entirely on how to achieve more by using MindManager. Newly improved in 2008, the eNewsletter is more colorful and compelling than the previous version. At the same time, it contains just as much useful content designed to make existing customers smarter users, and attract new users into the MindManager fold.

The eNewsletter makes excellent use of carefully chosen images that represent the concept, topic, or MindMap featured in each article. Each article features a succinct and descriptive headline, and just enough text to lure you into reading the entire article, downloading a mind map, or watching a video. For example, there is a video that shows how to link and attach documents. When you head off to watch the video, you have the opportunity to look at even more videos designed to help you become more productive when using MindManager software.

In addition, there are more Customer Columns, which feature content provided by subject matter experts. A recent issue presented ideas for strategic brainstorming and finding the perfect customer, and offered creativity methods that can be easily structured and reproduced. Each, of course, is presented with a mind map.

Although the content is 100% customer-centric, the eNewsletter offers you multiple opportunities to upgrade to the latest version of MindManager.

This eNewsletter illustrates the power of integrating relevant content with thoughtful visual design. The combination of images and text makes it much more likely that you will take action to go from the eNewsletter to the website. Each time you do so, Mindjet becomes essential in your eyes as a current or future supplier of productivity-enhancing tools.

Content Marketing Creates a Blockbuster Product Launch

In early 2007, Mindjet was ready to launch version 7.0 of MindManager. The biggest challenge was that relatively few analysts or media professionals are familiar with the concept of mindmapping, not to mention the product, MindManager.

The marketing team decided to create a precisely targeted mindmap that would be truly relevant to reporters and analysts. Rather than produce a PowerPoint presentation with a billion bullet points, they developed a mindmap that was all about how to write an article in the world of Web 2.0.

For example, the map showed how to use an RSS feed to stay current on topics related to mindmapping. In fact, the map contained two live links to RSS feed tools on the web. The mindmap was full of put-it-to-work-now tips, resources, and how-to's.

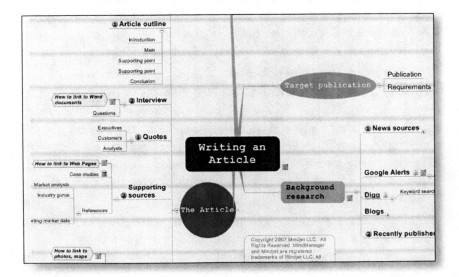

Chapter Seventeen:
Using Content Marketing to Accelerate the
Acceptance of a Concept and a Product

The genius of this strategy was that it made mindmapping not just understandable, but truly relevant to jaded and skeptical reporters and analysts, most of whom have suffered through thousands of never-ending PowerPoint presentations. Although the targeted mindmap was used for in-person presentations, it is also available for reporters over the Internet.

Did it work? Absolutely! Mindjet received more than 4,000 blog links and 232 media mentions. Perhaps most importantly, there are now hundreds of reporters around the world who understand what mindmapping is all about—and why MindManager is such a powerful product. Almost certainly, Mindjet won some converts among reporters who are actually leveraging MindManager to improve their productivity.

Content Marketing Takeaways

Word-of-mouth marketing has always been important. Today, it's more important than ever because of the power of the Internet. Mindjet employs a content marketing strategy designed to maximize word-of-mouth.

Mindjet understands that its customers love the MindManager product—and that they will use it more extensively and promote it more actively—if they are regularly exposed to all of its capabilities.

Thus, Mindjet uses its eNewsletter and its webcasts to demonstrate how MindManager can be used in a myriad of ways to improve professional and personal productivity.

Mindjet content creations are easy to pass along from one user to another. This gives real substance to word-of-mouth.

Mindjet used highly targeted and relevant content in its product launch so that reporters and analysts would intuitively understand how MindManager works and why it can be so powerful. Rather than issuing a standard press release that would be widely ignored, Mindjet put in a substantial amount of effort to create an elaborate mindmap that actually showed how to write an article. ❖

Chapter Eighteen:
Preserving the Value of Content

Content marketing provides 90% of the value of the
Webkinz product, but will Ganz risk it by placing ads at
Webkinz.com?

Type of Organization: Privately held Canadian toy manufacturer selling more than $100 million of Webkinz toy animals.

Major Marketing Objective: To create an interactive online community, Webkinz World, that supports the ongoing, increasing sales of its Webkinz stuffed animals.

Content Types:

» Website

Unique Element: Although the physical products are toy animals, almost all the value comes from the existence of the highly interactive online website that kids love and parents trust.

Results: Perceived value of its relatively expensive toys is created by superb kid-friendly online content marketing. Parents are paying-up because of the quality of the online content.

For those of you not familiar with Webkinz, they are very similar to what Cabbage Patch dolls were in the '80s except they are integrated with the Internet. Webkinz, owned by Toronto-based Ganz, are small stuffed dogs, pandas, cats, ducks, and other animals. Once the owner "adopts" their pet, they can go to the Webkinz website to register the pet, create a name, and bring their pet to life online.

The Webkinz concept is so simple, it boggles the mind that no one had thought of it earlier. To experience its power, just watch a four-year-old navigate his or her way through the site. You have to see it to believe it.

Here are a couple of points specific to the website and content marketing:

» The Webkinz site may be one of the greatest examples of a successful content marketing website in the world.

» Because the role of content marketing is so critical to Webkinz's success, Ganz risks disaster if it impairs the purity of the content with obtrusive advertising.

The Webkinz Business Model

According to a *BusinessWeek* article entitled "Toys with a Second Life" (December 20, 2007), Webkinz annual sales are north of $100 million. The revenues come strictly from the sale of its stuffed toys and accessories such as charms and clothes. Frankly, the stuffed animals are no different than what you'd find at any toy shop in the world. The difference is the Webkinz World online community.

The site is wonderfully constructed for both parents and kids.

It answers all the questions parents might have about safety, managing a child's time on the site, how it serves as an educational tool, and even what to do if a Webkinz pet gets sick.

Kids who are new to the site get a lively tour that explains how to register their pet and how to keep it happy, healthy, and busy in Webkinz World.

The image shown here is a real-world example of the Webkinz experience. Here you see Joe's six-year-old son Joshua's Webkinz, a polar bear named (fittingly) Polar. Joshua (as well as his younger brother Adam) has spent a good chunk of time on the Webkinz site fitting his animals with clothes, toys, carpet and wallpaper for the bedroom, and more. Joshua takes Polar to the doctor, to the exercise room, and to other "social" rooms where Polar can play with other Webkinz pets. Joshua needs to go to the store to buy food for Polar that will keep him healthy, and also has to play Webkinz games as a "job" in order to make money to buy more food, clothes, and toys for Polar.

As veteran marketer and mom Marie Kroesen Connell says:

> *"From a parental perspective, it's an excellent way to extend what they learn in school without it being a 'lesson.' My kids are constantly telling me what they are doing on the site, because they are so excited about what they buy or which friends they can interact with."*

It truly is a wonderfully educational and "sticky" site, and perhaps the best example we can think of for online content marketing. Webkinz World is *not* the product; it's the retention and growth mechanism. But it ultimately is the reason the brand is what it is today. The online component includes FREE content that educates its customer base and motivates buyers to buy more Webkinz products. Having more pets means your pets can play with one another, and also opens up exclusive items for multiple pet owners.

Webkinz has done what every business in the world seeks to do with its online content, yet it has so-integrated the product and the content that it seems indistinguishable. *What actually is the product? The toys or the online experience?* That is where Webkinz has perfected the art of content marketing.

When the content you produce for your customers becomes crucial to the success of the product itself, you have achieved perfect content marketing integration.

Could They Kill the Golden Webkinz?

Webkinz recently received a slew of hate mail from parents around the world when Ganz decided to open up a small amount of advertising on the site. This created a serious public relations problem for Ganz. Although it has taken the advertising down (such as ads for Jerry Seinfeld's *Bee Movie*), the company is still considering permitting advertising on the site for "kid-friendly" products.

We can see the storm coming now.

Judging by statements made in the *Business Week* article mentioned above, it seems that Ganz's managers—as well as financial experts—just do not "get" the true nature of the Webkinz World site:

> *"Ganz, which doesn't disclose its financials, must now strike a delicate balance: maximizing profit from the fad without alienating parents and kids. Visitors to Webkinz.com spent more than a million hours there in November, but the site is free. As a result, 'they haven't made anywhere near as much money as you'd think,' says Sean McGowan, an analyst at Needham, who guesses Webkinz sales are north of $100 million. He adds that none of the nascent competitors have figured out how to capitalize on kids' web time, either."*

The sales are north of $100 million because Ganz created a safe and educational website that parents can leave their kids on without having to worry.

As Marie Kroesen Connell notes:

> *"I think the executives at Webkinz are trying to see what other avenues of income they can derive by modifying their business model. With traffic to its web site increasing exponentially, it is tempting for Webkinz to find a way to capitalize on it financially. I can't blame them. But it would seem to me, that it is*

> *important not to alienate their loyal customers who go there for
> the Webkinz content, not ads for other companies."*

In other words, it's all about the content.

Webkinz has grown because it is delivering high-quality, FREE content, with the expectation that the website will drive more Webkinz sales, not that the website will produce revenue itself.

Opening up web advertising, no matter how kid-friendly, threatens the brand and diminishes the value of the site. Playhouse Disney opened its website to advertising a few years ago. That was the same time Joe stopped allowing his kids to go to that site. Joe's kids clicked on those ads like crazy and ended up heaven knows where. Disney forgot that the website was not there to make money, but to deepen the brand relationship—i.e., get customers to watch more Playhouse Disney and buy more Disney toys.

If the management team at Ganz asked us (and they haven't), we would strongly advise them that Webkinz needs to keep its site advertising-free—or it will destroy the safe environment it has created for children. As we go to press, Ganz is only offering "house" ads related to Webkinz products and not outside advertising.

Content Marketing Takeaways

All businesses need to create their own content channels, as Webkinz has. Most businesses don't realize that they can create their own online resource centers for customers that will ultimately drive loyalty and sales. Miller Electric has done it with MillerWelds.com (see Chapter Eight). Consumer or business-to-business… doesn't matter. Just create content that meets the informational needs of your buyer, treat it for what it is, and watch what it can do.

When content marketing products succeed, such as online content websites or custom publishing print magazines, brands almost instinctively want to open those channels up to advertising. This is almost always a bad idea. Opening up other messages dilutes what you are trying to communicate to your customer. You also lose more control, as Playhouse Disney did when its customers clicked on other websites, alienating parents in the process.

The best content marketing doesn't have to be online. In the Webkinz case, it clearly is. Others might be in print or in-person. It's most likely a combination of the three. Successful content programs meet the customers where they are. If you can do all three, it makes the content come alive that much more. ❖

Chapter Nineteen:
ThomasNet—A Content Marketer's Content Marketer

Making the online leap, ThomasNet bet everything on the Internet. But its customers' websites weren't ready for the new buying paradigm. Now, ThomasNet uses online and in-person content marketing to help thousands of customers succeed with the new breed of industrial buyer.

Type of Organization: Online division of large, 110-year-old private publishing company.

Major Marketing Objective: To grow its online revenues by using targeted, relevant, and valuable content to help its readers and customers succeed.

Content Types:

» Website

» Microsite

» In-person workshops

» Online directory

» Online product news site

» eNewsletter

Unique Element: ThomasNet had to find a way to teach its small- to medium-sized clients how to use content effectively in order to sell successfully online. Its clients' success was essential to its success.

Results: ThomasNet has helped hundreds of clients succeed. This, in turn, has made its 100% online content strategy succeed.

I f you're not immersed in the world of manufacturing, you may not have noticed the disappearance of the venerable *Thomas Register*. This green-printed, shelf-filling directory is now 100% online.

Thomas Publishing Company, creator of the *Thomas Register* is 110 years old in 2008. It was a pioneer at the end of the nineteenth century—and it's still a pioneer today.

The original concept was to provide comprehensive and current product information for manufacturers as the U.S. transitioned from an agricultural to an industrial economy.

Created in 1898 by Henry Mark Thomas, the *Thomas Register* grew to include product information on 650,000 distributors and manufacturers covering more than 67,000 industrial categories. If you have ever called on an industrial purchasing agent, you have almost certainly seen bookshelves full of the distinctive green directories behind the desk.

Actually, Thomas Publishing was a twentieth-century pioneer in several other important areas. The company invented the first product news tabloid magazine and the reader service card. Both kept buyers current on products and provided them an efficient way to request product and service information.

In the old days—say the early '90s—the buying process remained pretty much as it had been for a hundred years. The *Thomas Register*, product news tabloids, and reader service cards worked just as they always had.

While in the planning stages, buyers would request information about products they had seen in magazines or had rooted out in the *Thomas Register*. They still called vendors to determine whether they had appropriate products. Vendors would then send product literature, which might have been outdated the day it was printed. Finally, a sales rep would probably call to see if the purchaser was ready to make a buying decision. A substantial percentage of this pre-purchase research was done by contacting the vendor directly.

All this represented a comfortable and familiar process for the small- to medium-sized manufacturers that make up the bulk of industrial companies in the U.S.

By the early 2000s, the ubiquity and functionality of the Internet changed the product research landscape. Buyers began to operate differently. Increasingly, they were conducting their research exclusively online. They were able to gather most of what they needed before they ever contacted the manufacturer directly.

The Internet enabled the creation of ThomasNet (ThomasNet.com) to provide truly current and comprehensive product information for manufacturers in an online version. Even better, ThomasNet could provide additional online services that would help its customers sell more products more efficiently.

Ever the pioneer, the Thomas Industrial Network, a Thomas Publishing business unit, killed off the venerable *Register* in 2006. It gambled that by putting all of its efforts behind a powerful online directory, ThomasNet.com, it would not only replace lost print revenues, but would find new revenue opportunities.

The online version offers incredible functionality that far surpasses its late print predecessor. ThomasNet considers itself a "destination site" where buyers come for the explicit purpose of finding the products they need and the vendors that can supply them.

In fact, ThomasNet is the most logical place on the web to look for products and services that relate to manufacturing. Even though you could probably search on Google for the same thing, it would be highly inefficient—and ultimately yield lots of useless results. Why go elsewhere? After all, according to the company:

> *"ThomasNet.com is the one-stop destination that enables users to find the exact product, service, or supplier they need, at the exact time they need it. Through ThomasNet.com, buyers also have instant access to the detailed information they need to make a purchasing or specifying decision, including line-item product details, supplier product catalogs, CAD drawings, and more.*

So far, so good.

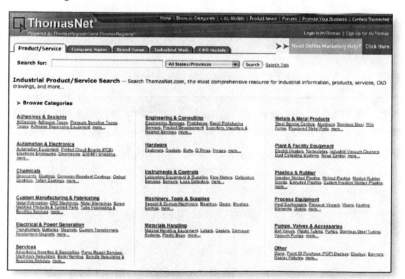

After its first year online, however, ThomasNet faced an unexpected problem: Although it drove lots of traffic to its customers' websites, hundreds of customers were canceling their advertising.

Here's what they found:

Although ThomasNet was sending thousands of highly qualified visitors to clients, that's all these prospects were doing—visiting. They weren't buying. Why?

The answer was deceptively simple. The majority of client websites were not designed to make it easy for visitors to become buyers. Because most of ThomasNet's clients were small- to medium-sized businesses, they were not typically web-savvy. Nor did they have huge online budgets. Moreover, there was no proven model for success. The changed buying process was just too new.

ThomasNet Teaches Advertisers How to Build Websites that Make It Easy to Buy

As soon as ThomasNet understood the problem, it got to work creating a solution. The marketing team conducted research about online business-to-business buying patterns to determine what elements are critical to a successful site. It turned out that real content is essential. Without it, visitors will make a brief stop, get frustrated by a lack of substance, leave, and then probably won't return.

Alienating prospective buyers is potentially disastrous. Why? Because websites provide the overwhelming majority of information about potential suppliers and their products!

Buyers don't have time to gab with salespeople anymore. They have very little leisure time at all. They are under the gun to deliver results now. So, your website needs to make their job easy. They have to know that you have what they need and that you are a company they would like to buy from.

For ThomasNet, everything boiled down to a single question: "Does your website persuade visitors to become customers?" If not, you lose. If yes, you have an excellent chance to succeed.

Here is how Linda Rigano, director of strategic alliances, Thomas Industrial Network, explains it:

> *"Your website needs to serve as your 24/7 salesperson. It needs to inform and persuade a visitor to become a customer. If it doesn't, your visitors will make a brief stop, hit the back button,*

and never return. You may never know. We learned that driving traffic to ThomasNet.com and to our advertisers' websites wasn't enough. We had to help our clients develop meaningful content and tools that can be implemented easily and economically. ThomasNet's business model has been instrumental in helping our clients succeed. In the end, it's all about providing content that makes it easy for customers to buy."

Fortunately for its advertisers, ThomasNet was able to develop a formula to guide the creation of websites that make it easy to buy. They call it V.S.E.T.:

» **Verify** that you offer the products they need—Does your website make it easy for potential customers to immediately determine whether you have what they are looking for?

» **Search** for specific products—Can buyers search your website in multiple ways (e.g., by part number, keyword, or product specifications)?

» **Evaluate** your product offerings—Do you provide buyers with enough detailed information so they can make a buying decision? Can they compare products side-by-side? Or do you offer CAD drawings for them to download, if applicable?

» **Take Action**—Do you offer multiple ways for buyers to request more information from you or buy from you, including contact information, RFQ links, your phone number on every page, or even e-commerce?

Microsite Provides a Deep Reservoir of Content that Teaches Content Marketing

ThomasNet provides a very useful microsite, PromoteYourBusiness.ThomasNet.com. You don't have to be a customer to use the microsite—and you don't have to use ThomasNet's marketing services to benefit from the knowledge you gain from exploring it. This is an excellent example of content marketing at work.

The primary objective of the microsite is to make ThomasNet's customers smarter about how to manage their own content marketing efforts. Visitors can also access practical white papers that give them a more in-depth understanding of how to create a content-rich website, how to drive traffic, and how to integrate content marketing with a business plan. Of course, ThomasNet does make it easy for visitors to contact them to pursue the purchase of products and services. Yet, none of this takes away from the intrinsic value of the information that ThomasNet provides.

Advertisers who have built or rebuilt websites that follow the V.S.E.T. methodology have achieved dramatic increases in web-based sales.

For example, Flex Products, a small plastics packaging company with $3.5 million in 2005 sales had never spent more than $5,000 on promotion—all of it in the old *Thomas Register*. It saw a decline in the effectiveness of trade shows and was looking for alternatives. So it turned to ThomasNet for the creation of an online catalog.

In less than two years, the results were spectacular. Sales jumped to $10 million. Fifty-percent of those sales came from the company's new web catalog. For Flex Products, it boiled down to having really useful and relevant content online. The company was able to show not only what it stocked, but the kinds of custom products that it could produce.

ThomasNet Puts In-Person Content Marketing to Work

Although it might seem counterintuitive, Rigano and her team spend much of their time on the road conducting workshops with veteran manufacturing executives. Their objective is to teach these grizzled manufacturing veterans exactly how to put V.S.E.T. methodology to work.

In fact, these workshops represent another very important form of content marketing. The ThomasNet team has come to understand that, for many of its customers, the web learning curve is pretty darned steep. These clients rarely have an intuitive understanding of the magnitude of buying behavior changes—and how essential it is that they transform their web presence. The industrial buying process has changed so dramatically that ThomasNet customers and their companies have to relearn how to connect with their own customers in the U.S. and around the world.

Content Marketing Takeaways

The fundamental changes in buyer behavior that we have discussed elsewhere in this book have had an earth-shattering impact in the industrial marketplace.

Engineers and purchasing executives rely on the Internet for more than 90% of the product research they conduct prior to purchase. Therefore, vendors must utilize content marketing effectively so they are under consideration during the 24/7 online research process.

In this marketplace, content does not need to be fancy, but it does need to be comprehensive, easy to find, and easy to use. The Flex Products catalog site is a perfect example. It's not elegant, but it is extremely easy to use and has resulted in a dramatic increase in the company's product sales.

Flex Products is simply one of hundreds of ThomasNet clients that have benefited from successful content marketing implementations.

Since 1898, Thomas Publishing has been all about providing current and comprehensive content. Today, it has taken the next step and is teaching its customers how to provide current and comprehensive content. In that way, when ThomasNet succeeds, its customers succeed. ❖

Chapter Twenty:
E-mail Software Provider Teaches Customers to Market Effectively

Constant Contact really walks the walk when it comes to content marketing.

Type of Organization: Newly public supplier of e-mail management and online research software.

Major Marketing Objective: To grow usage of its software products by helping its customers succeed with effective e-mail marketing.

Content Types:

» Website

» eNewsletter

» Webcasts

» In-person workshops

Unique Element: Constant Contact cannot succeed unless its customers succeed; it must provide relevant and valuable content in order to grow.

Results: The company is growing users, usage, and revenues dramatically. Content marketing is at the heart of that growth.

This fast-growing company probably doesn't attribute all of its recent growth acceleration to content marketing. But having observed the company over several years, as customers while working in different organizations, we realized that it has significantly improved its content marketing skills. Our guess is that its 87% third quarter 2007 vs. 2006 year-over-year growth can be attributed, at least in part, to its effective implementation of a comprehensive content marketing strategy.

Today, Constant Contact does an excellent job of content marketing on its website and, of course, via e-mail. But, interestingly, it also does a great job of in-person content marketing via its regional representatives.

The company targets small- to medium-sized businesses that want to grow revenues by marketing more effectively. These targeted companies need to leverage their limited resources both with affordable tools and with best marketing practices. Constant Contact provides the tools and teaches best practices.

Constant Contact understands that its 150,000+ customers need to communicate effectively in order to grow. It also knows that most of its customers are not sophisticated marketing experts—and almost certainly are not e-mail marketing experts. Therefore, Constant Contact provides very practical, nuts-and-bolts teaching that empowers its customers to be successful through the use of its tools and through best practices in terms of e-mail marketing and e-mail-based research. Eric Groves, the company's senior vice president of sales and business development, explains it this way:

> *"No matter how a customer wants to learn, we strive to provide an educational experience that meets their needs. We recognize that everyone learns not only in different ways, but at different times. To help educate and support our customers' needs, we offer seminars, webinars, how-to guides, newsletters, and a blog. This is complemented by our free, live support via phone, e-mail, and text chat."*

Current Website Shows Intense Content Marketing Focus

A quick look at Constant Contact's circa 2004 website on the Internet Wayback machine (Archive.org) shows a dramatic shift to a comprehensive content marketing strategy on the January 2008 iteration. The old website did a good job of explaining what the product did and how it worked. It even offered some solid case studies to prove that Constant Contact's e-mail software worked. But it did relatively little to turn neophyte e-mail marketers into experts.

The big difference between the old website and the new website is its obvious focus on making its customers successful.

From the get-go, this company makes it absolutely clear how it can help you solve your marketing problems:

> *"No matter what size your organization, you can rely on Constant Contact to help you create e-mail campaigns and online surveys that build lasting relationships with your customers, members, or clients."*

Within a few seconds you can determine exactly what Constant Contact does and how it can help you. It invites you to take a tour. It shows you how inexpensive the software is. And it offers you a free 60-day trial—no credit card required!

Also on the homepage is a link to live webinars that teach you how to be effective by mastering basic e-mail marketing best practices, such as:

» Building better lists

» Subject line design

» Creating marketing e-mails

» eNewsletter makeover

» Planning a survey

It also provides lots of recorded video tutorials that teach even more core concepts.

Constant Contact offers a series of white papers that may be just what you need to convince management that it needs to get more serious about content marketing. These papers cover topics such as "why you need to create an eNewsletter" and "how to keep your customers with e-mail."

Of course, Constant Contact wouldn't be really walking the walk unless it also did a great job creating its own compelling eNewsletters.

Great Customer-Centric eNewsletters

The strength of Constant Contact's eNewsletter has to do with its content and clean design—even though it probably has a marketing budget most of us would die for. However, we can all afford to replicate the style and sophistication of this newsletter, even if we are small business executives with micro-budgets.

Constant Contact's software? Inexpensive. Its eNewsletter content? Invaluable.

Here's what you can learn from *Hints & Tips Email Marketing*:

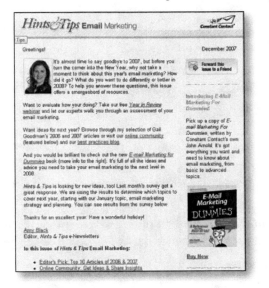

Content-rich eNewsletters are one of the most effective marketing tools in the Internet age. But they won't work unless you carefully target the most pressing information needs of your prospective customers.

Constant Contact's eNewsletter is typically packed with information that is relevant to its target customers. Here are some samples from past issues:

> » A focused "Year in Review Webinar" that helped subscribers evaluate the success of their e-mail marketing programs. Of course, it was free to subscribers.

> » Links to live webinars, the company's blog, and to a place where readers can buy the book *E-Mail Marketing for Dummies* written by marketing trainer John Arnold, the company's regional development director.

> » An editor's choice of Top 10 articles from 2006 and 2007, including:

>   • Why am I getting this? Making e-mail communication relevant to the receiver.

>   • Ask and you shall succeed. Using online surveys to improve your e-mail communications.

>   • Five steps to creating better e-mail campaigns.

>   • Getting the subject line right.

» A connection to Constant Contact's online community, ConnectUp!

» 2007 reader survey results.

A simple, easy-to-follow design

Constant Contact's eNewsletter is very simple with relatively few graphics. It gets right to the point and provides relevant links to a broad range of information resources. While scrolling, you just keep getting more and more information. When you go to the editor's Top 10 article picks, you see a one-paragraph summary of each article with a link to click on if you want to read the entire article. The paragraph gives you just enough information to decide whether or not you want to click on the link.

Extending In-Person Content Marketing All Over the U.S.

Newt had the opportunity to participate in a marketing workshop with Lisa Sparks, Constant Contact's regional director for South Florida, at the Greater Naples Chamber of Commerce. The attendees were precisely the type of small business owners and executives that Constant Contact targets. They were hungry for information about how to leverage the Internet and e-mail to market their organizations more effectively.

Lisa is an excellent speaker, knowledgeable about small business marketing topics and, of course, about e-mail marketing. She spends much of her time at events like this where she can share knowledge about the use of effective e-mail marketing to attract and retain customers. When asked how much of her business comes from this highly effective in-person content marketing strategy, she replied, "80%."

And, of course, she has her own monthly eNewsletter that provides practical advice about marketing more effectively. It also provides links to great resources and free tools.

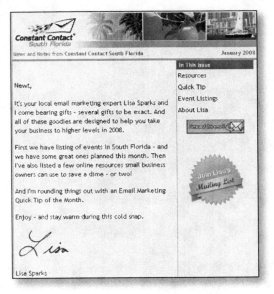

This Company Actually Uses What It Sells!

Constant Contact eats its own dog food! These folks use the software they sell to demonstrate how to communicate effectively via e-mail and eNewsletters.

By making very good use of its own products, the company proves in the most obvious way that e-mail marketing works—and that its products work. No marketing strategy is more effective than proving that the products you sell enable you to sell more products.

Content Marketing Takeaways

When your success ultimately depends directly on your clients' success, content marketing that enables them to succeed is not only a great strategy, it may be the only strategy that makes sense.

Turning your customers into experts in the use of your products to grow their businesses will make them your best salespeople.

In-person content marketing works brilliantly when you provide information that solves your customers' problems—and secondarily involves the use of your products.

You can conduct sophisticated e-mail marketing campaigns without a significant dollar investment.

A website that is all about helping its customers succeed will pull in both new visitors and returning customers.

When you're selling a technology product, make it very, very easy for your customers to try it for free. ❖

Chapter Twenty-One:
UK Law Firm Uses Content Marketing to Build Powerful New Brand

Type of Organization: 1,000-lawyer legal firm with HQ in London.

Major Marketing Objectives:

>> To be the biggest legal brand on the web

>> To replace traditional marketing with content marketing

>> To generate demonstrable return on marketing investment

Content Types:

>> Website

>> Weekly eNewsletter

>> RSS feeds

>> Semi-annual print magazine

>> Podcasts

Unique Element: Created a dedicated content team in 2000 that drives a coherent, consistent complement of content, both in print and online.

Results: Multi-million-dollar return on relatively small content marketing investment.

If you thought all British law firms were stodgy and old-fashioned, you haven't yet encountered Pinsent Masons. The only thing old-fashioned about this firm is its name. In fact, it has been doing online and print content marketing for nearly a decade.

The firm's website, Out-Law.com, provides a wealth of timely and useful content for its current and prospective clients. In addition, it produces a semi-annual print publication, also called *Out-Law*. Neither information product is the kind of very traditional marketing you would expect from a venerable global law firm. But that's because this team understood from the beginning that great content was fundamental to building a great brand.

Back in 2000, before the dot-com implosion, this law firm and many of its peers in the UK launched websites. Most of the others dropped by the wayside or contented themselves with brochure-style websites.

The common thread of the also-rans was that they failed to provide relevant content. Because they relied on overworked lawyers to provide the content, they lacked the single-minded focus required to drive a successful content marketing strategy. After all, when your responsibility is to generate billable hours, spending time writing articles for a website just doesn't make much sense.

Pinsent Masons took a much different tack. From the beginning, it made a number of very smart decisions that have been effectively executed by its content marketing team:

» Although it has 1,000 lawyers, the firm realized that it had to form a dedicated content team if it really wanted quality content. So, in May 2000, it hired Struan Robertson, who is both a lawyer and an excellent writer. From the outset, his entire job responsibility has revolved around the firm's content marketing efforts.

» It chose a slightly edgy name to brand its website, Out-Law.com. It was meant to evoke a slight feeling of the American Wild West to suggest outside-the-box thinking. The name is also easy to remember and easy to find via search engines.

» Its content is tightly focused on technology law. It is crystal-clear on its positioning:

   • It seeks to provide everything about the law for technology firms.

   • It seeks to provide everything about technology law for other firms.

» Soon after Struan was hired, the organization added a full-time professional journalist to ensure that the content would be client-centered.

» The writers always write like business journalists, because they know that a high percentage of their current and future clients are business executives, not lawyers. They have also learned that even lawyers enjoy great journalism.

» They do real reporting, including interviews with high-level executives and technology experts. In early 2008, they scooped a number of publications by interviewing a European browser maker who was about to take on Microsoft in court.

Before 2000, the firm's marketing was conventional. As Struan puts it, "We were producing thousands of boring brochures that recipients tossed upon receipt." The firm was unable to attribute any significant return on this brochure investment. It was producing brochures because that's what it had always done.

Three team members, attorneys John Salmon and Jon Fell, joined by marketing manager Vincent Gray, decided it was time for some significant marketing changes. They originated the idea for a website that would deliver valuable content that their current and future clients would actually want to read.

Website Reaches 120,000 Visitors Per Month

Online, the firm's goal is simple and ambitious: *"To be the biggest legal brand on the web."* After nearly a decade of continuous improvement, it may well have nailed that goal. In its first year on the web, it averaged just 1,000 visitors per month. In 2007, it attracted 1.4 million visitors over the course of the year. That's a 10,000% increase!

The website is very much news-driven, delivering three to five new stories every day. Overall, the site contains more than 8,000 articles on technology law and on law for technology companies.

The site is well-organized, providing a wealth of logically structured information, including:

» Guides on specific topics

» Articles divided into more than two dozen categories

» Articles sorted by the ultimate applications such as startups, financial services, media and entertainment, and interactive media

» In-depth case studies that explore some of the most pressing technology law issues

» Information on the variety of services provided

» Who they are and why you might want to do business with them

» Who to contact when you're ready to do business

Almost all of the content on Out-Law.com is customer-centric. It is carefully designed to make its readers more knowledgeable about legal issues within the firm's areas of expertise. The website makes it very easy to find exactly what you're looking for.

The firm is now also making all of its content available for PDAs and other mobile devices. That way you can find exactly what you need even when you're on the run.

Weekly eNewsletter Directs 15,000 Subscribers Back to Website

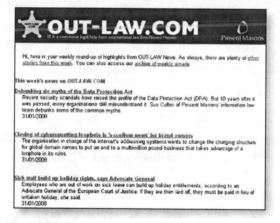

Starting in 2000, the firm also created a weekly eNewsletter that now reaches 15,000 subscribers. It provides quick summaries of the top six stories of the week, which link back to website. In addition, you can click on a link that takes you back to last month's stories.

Other than its header, which focuses on the Out-Law.com sheriff's badge logo, the newsletter has no graphical elements at all. It's designed to be a very quick read that enables its recipients to decide whether they want to pursue a particular article or move on with their day.

The eNewsletter is archived on the website going back to the beginning of 2007. In addition, you can choose to receive it via RSS feed. It has a smart and client-centric twist to RSS: It makes 10 different RSS feeds available that focus on specific legal and technology topics.

Pinsent Masons Has Been Podcasting Since August 2006

Although business-related podcasting is relatively new, the firm was characteristically a pioneer. Just as the team has been careful to operate more as business journalists than as lawyers, so, too, has it approached podcasting.

The weekly podcasts are treated like commercial business radio broadcasts that you might expect in the U.S. from NPR, ABC, or CNN. The objective is to conduct interesting or relevant interviews with experts who can provide unique insights to podcast listeners. Of course, the podcasts are linked both from the eNewsletter and the website.

Recent Research Shows Tangible Content Marketing Results

In a recent e-mail survey that generated an impressive 700 responses, Pinsent Masons made some important discoveries about its website visitors:

» 38% are decision makers

» 96% plan to contact Pinsent Masons

» 63% found the law firm via the web

» Only 14% were existing clients

More importantly, the firm is confident that it can track millions of British pounds' worth of business to its online content marketing efforts.

Relevant Magazine Replaces Ineffective Brochures

When a law firm puts Homer Simpson on the cover of its magazine, *Out-Law.com Magazine*, you know it's doing something very different from its peers. As Struan says, "We set out to design a magazine that you would want to pick up on the newsstand." With Homer on the cover, how could you *not* pick it up?

More than 10,500 targeted clients have requested copies. An additional 7,000 are handed out at industry events each year.

The firm strives to make the magazine as interesting and compelling as any high-quality business journal. The content is written for CEOs, CFOs, and COOs—not for lawyers.

Pinsent Masons does an excellent job of integrating the magazine's content with high-impact graphics that enhance the readability of the feature articles. This is not a law journal—it's an enjoyable business publication that just happens to cover topics about technology law.

The content team has been very clever with its use of high-profile entertainment images (e.g., pictures of Homer Simpson and actor Matt Damon) by approaching studios that are in the process of releasing films. Not only don't they have to pay high prices for great art work, they get it for *free* from studios that are only too happy for the extra promotion. Brilliant.

A recent issue of *OutLaw.com Magazine* covered topics including:

» The potential assault on personal privacy by mega-technology companies

» The unfortunate import of class-action litigation from the U.S. to Europe

» The danger of trampling on basic consumer expectations in a Web 2.0 world

» The risks posed by "typo infringement" of your website address by cyber squatters

» A company's legal responsibility in the face of a security breach

The magazine also has a lively mailbag section with spirited responses from readers to magazine content.

Each of these topics could have been treated in a boring fashion and written in pedantic legalese. Instead, the editors write in a comfortable, colloquial style that reminds us of how wittily articulate our British cousins can be. Here's a snippet from the article about personal privacy:

> *"These are companies with so much personal information about us that they see into the darkest reaches of our souls more clearly than Sigmund Freud channeled by Mystic Meg. They are peopled by zealous superbrains who doodle weather system algorithms while chatting to granny on the phone, yet even they can't decide on the right way to handle our personal data."*

Out-Law.com Magazine is an unexpected pleasure, full of well-written articles enhanced by professional design and compelling graphics.

Great Content Marketing Has Replaced Old-Fashioned Ways of Communicating with Clients

Because of its single-minded focus on delivering great content, Pinsent Masons has avoided spending money on unproductive marketing efforts into which most of its competitors are still pouring out large sums of money. This has proved to be both a smart and cost-effective approach.

Apart from staffing, other costs are minimal. Because it has a sophisticated content management system, the firm can manage all of its online efforts in-house. The most expensive components of its twice-yearly magazine are printing and mailing. The art budget is just $600 per year.

Pinsent Masons does no other advertising beyond its website, eNewsletter, podcasts, and magazine. In fact, it is able to "trade" promotion in its online or print vehicles for trade show booths and other event sponsorships.

Today, the Out-Law.com brand stands for technology law leadership. It is recognized by thousands and thousands of web visitors, eNewsletter readers, and magazine subscribers. This unique and powerful brand enables Pinsent Masons to stand out from the hundreds of other firms whose names still come from those of long-dead partners.

As indicated earlier, this firm has been able to track millions of pounds' worth of business to its integrated content marketing efforts. Moreover, because it does no other advertising or direct marketing, it knows that its content marketing strategy is its most important growth driver.

Content Marketing Takeaways

Even a small, dedicated content creation team can make all the difference when it comes to providing relevant and valuable information. Because it has a single-minded focus, Pinsent Masons' team of talented and motivated professionals has been able to outperform an army of lawyers in other firms who have been drafted to create articles. These legal conscripts lacked either the time, inclination, or talent—or all three—to provide timely and consistent content.

A business organization can build a brand with a carefully chosen name that comes to symbolize a wealth of valuable content that, in turn, reinforces the quality of its people, products, and services.

In the business-to-business arena, it is possible to completely abandon traditional marketing with a well-planned and well-executed content marketing strategy.

A small content marketing investment within a company of any size can deliver returns disproportionate to the level of investment. Once a basic content marketing infrastructure has been created, delivering that content can be both less expensive and more effective than paying for an advertising presence within traditional media outlets. ❖

Chapter Twenty-Two:
Rockwell Automation Uses Content Marketing to Be Global, Local, and Cost-Effective

This global manufacturing company goes way beyond promoting the "features" of its products and services, to clearly explaining how it provides solutions for its customers.

Type of Organization: $5 billion multi-national corporation with HQ in Milwaukee, Wisconsin.

Major Marketing Objective: To strengthen ties to Australian customers with an integrated print/online content marketing program that bridges cultures and languages.

Content Types:

» Print magazine

» eZines

» eNewsletters

» Comprehensive online product and service library

Unique Element: The Asia-Pacific marketing group creates a core publication in English that is customized by language and content to match local needs.

Results: Content-rich publications build trusted relationships with a diverse customer base by helping to solve problems and teach best practices.

You just know that a company whose service mark is *"Listen. Think. Solve."* will have a pretty good handle on content marketing. This global manufacturing company uses both print and online content marketing effectively to connect with its technically savvy buyers around the world.

Even with a limited budget, the Rockwell Automation Asia-Pacific division is able to reach out to customers and prospects in multiple languages and multiple ways. Traditional trade publication advertising has become less effective over the years. In addition, in the Asia-Pacific region, trade shows, which are big in North America and Europe, are relatively rare. This limits the ways in which this manufacturing giant can communicate effectively and regularly with its audience.

Because of these limitations, Rockwell has chosen to create its own high-quality content, which reflects the high quality of its products and services.

Custom Magazine Targeted to Specific Countries

Rockwell's Asia-Pacific magazine *Automation Today* is an excellent example of how to provide relevant content that is both broadly applicable to customers—and customized to individual countries. *Automation Today* typifies Rockwell's "Listen. Think. Solve.®" approach to its customers and to content marketing.

Gail Anderson, manager of Asia-Pacific marketing communications, notes that Rockwell's current approach is much different from the way it used to handle customer communications:

> "We used to be very feature-oriented and internally focused. But we have learned that our customers are looking for solutions. We now take a customer-centric selling approach to determine what our customers need to solve their problems."

Gail's comments about being customer-centric ring true on the web. Here's how the company describes what it does at the very top of its website's homepage:

> "When it comes to automation, your requirements are unique. So are our solutions. We listen to you, then apply our resources to build cost-effective, results-based solutions. It could be a single, powerful component. An information or asset management solution. Or an enterprise-wide, integrated system. Whatever your automation requirement, you'll find the answer by partnering with us."

Rockwell Automation is a $5 billion global company with 20,000 employees worldwide, serving customers in 80 countries. It provides solutions both to manufacturing end-users and to OEMs. According to the company, these solutions are "designed to give our customers a competitive edge."

In fact, Rockwell Automation is a veteran content marketer and has long published a monthly magazine in North America called *The Journal.* This magazine is very much customer- and solution-focused. Although *The Journal* is a custom publication, it could certainly stand on its own as a solid monthly manufacturing magazine.

Automation Today stands on the shoulders of its North American sister publication. Gail and her team launched the new magazine in 1999 to provide relevant and meaningful content to a diverse audience of customers in the Asia-Pacific region. Previously, it had simply mailed copies of *The Journal* from the U.S. This was less than optimal because it was expensive and because the magazine contained a great deal of North American advertising which had relatively little relevance to the Asia-Pacific market.

Although *Automation Today* can pick-up stories from its sister magazine, its content tends to be unique and specific to its own markets. To be certain that the publication is relevant to its readers, the team has conducted research asking whether it gives customer readers what they need; whether the articles are the right length; whether the frequency is right; and whether it's written to the right technical level. The team has also determined exactly who is reading the magazine and whether it's being shared with colleagues.

The magazine is prepared in electronic format with 18 fixed pages and two blank pages, which can be filled with local content. Some country teams actually add extra pages to the publication. It is printed in five languages: two versions in Chinese, plus Japanese, Korean, and British English. Each country manages its own final production, printing, and circulation.

Typical feature articles are fairly horizontal so that it is clear to readers in different disciplines how they can benefit from the solution described. Although many of the articles do feature Rockwell products and services, they are always written from the perspective of solving customer problems.

For example, a typically practical article described a three-step migration program that enables manufacturers to transition from aging distributed control systems ($65 billion worth of existing control systems are estimated to be near the end of their life-cycle). The process described is designed to eliminate most of the pain from a complex transition. Even though the process is illustrated with Rockwell Automation equipment, it would apply no matter what kind of automation equipment was involved.

more diagnostics. That diagnostic information can be leveraged in a manufacturer's asset management solution to drive down costs as part of a predictive maintenance strategy.

For example, the asset management functionality in the Integrated Architecture for Process Control spans from the process field device level to motor control centres. It includes comprehensive diagnostics, device configuration and calibration as well as real-time and operator audits.

Integrated Architecture for Process Control offers a redundant, high-availability system that is scalable from under 50 I/O points to over 50,000 I/O points.

Detailed and useful graphics accompany the more complex feature articles. Thus, an article about process control automation included a very detailed graphical diagram of the system and process described. It's obvious that a great deal of care has gone into each element of the magazine.

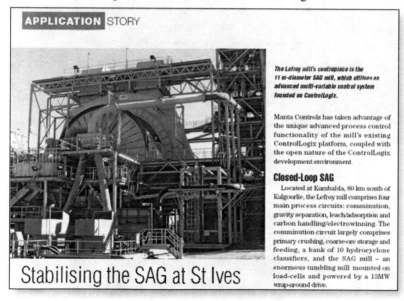

APPLICATION STORY

The Lefroy mill's centrepiece is the 11 m-diameter SAG mill, which utilises an advanced multi-variable control system founded on ControlLogix.

Manta Controls has taken advantage of the unique advanced process control functionality of the mill's existing ControlLogix platform, coupled with the open nature of the ControlLogix development environment.

Closed-Loop SAG

Located at Kambalda, 80 km south of Kalgoorlie, the Lefroy mill comprises four main process circuits: comminution, gravity separation, leach/adsorption and carbon handling/electrowinning. The comminution circuit largely comprises primary crushing, coarse-ore storage and feeding, a bank of 10 hydrocyclone classifiers, and the SAG mill – an enormous tumbling mill mounted on load-cells and powered by a 13MW wrap-around drive.

Stabilising the SAG at St Ives

Each issue also features a number of customer success stories. The October 2007 issue described an incredibly complex Rockwell Automation application in an Australian gold mine. It involved the implementation of an "expert control" system in a very challenging process control situation. The discussion of the implementation is sophisticated, high-level, and well-written.

The Australia Team Adds Valuable Content in Print and Online

Each country within the Asia-Pacific region can customize its content marketing efforts. The Australian team does an excellent job with its version of the magazine. It also publishes a useful and enjoyable eNewsletter.

The Australian team uses its two pages effectively so that it seems to their Australian customers that this is an outstanding local manufacturing magazine. For example, one of its brief articles, "A Day in the Life of a Technical Instructor," does a great job of humanizing a critical member of the Rockwell team, John Sciberras. By describing in detail what he does and how he does it, readers learn how a talented Rockwell veteran spends his time helping customers just like them to keep their technical knowledge and skills current.

The Aussie team does a great job of content marketing online as well. Its eNewsletter is delivered bimonthly and is promoted as "…packed with the most up-to-the-minute news…this eNewsletter will enable you to be among the first to find out about new products, training, services, events, workshops, and any special offers from Rockwell Automation Australia."

The December 2007 issue includes 10 articles on a wide variety of topics. Readers find everything from how to protect their automation investment, to asset management, to the complete 2008 training schedule.

The lead story highlights a group of Adelaide University students who have created an automated version of foosball that can blow away the human opposition. Several stories in the newsletter, including this one, feature local partners. In this way, the newsletter provides useful and interesting content to its end-users—and helps to promote the services of its trusted local partners.

Vital Global Customer Resource: The Corporate Online Literature Library

The Asia-Pacific team benefits from a well-structured corporate site that includes a wealth of product-related content to make it easier for customers to buy.

The Literature Library is a perfect example. It is clearly organized by:

» Products

» Industries and applications

» Services and support

» Solutions

Current and prospective customers can drill down to find an incredible amount of information about any product or service they are likely to need—and how it would be used in their application or industry. Thus, in a few minutes, buyers can access what would have taken many phone calls, lots of postage, and lots of time just five or 10 years ago. Rockwell Automation provides instant information gratification for its web visitors.

Content Marketing Takeaways

The Asia-Pacific division of Rockwell Automation has a limited marketing budget. It has chosen to focus much of its effort on content marketing because it accurately reflects the company's customer-centric focus.

When the folks at Rockwell talk about listening, thinking, and solving, they are dead-serious. The quality of their print and online publications makes it clear to their customers that Rockwell means what it says.

Rockwell's products and services provide solutions to thorny manufacturing problems. Its content marketing efforts focus on providing relevant information that describes how to solve those problems. Although its magazine's articles typically talk about Rockwell products and services, they have intrinsic value based on the thoroughness and clarity of their discussion of technical, process, and automation issues.

Rockwell Automation proves that just because you're a technology company doesn't mean that you have to live in a feature-oriented universe. In fact, customer-centric content marketing is probably even more important if this is the world in which you operate. If you can describe to your potential customers how they can stay at the top of their game technologically and how they can solve very difficult manufacturing problems, you will begin to earn their trust and show that you and your organization are the competent and caring partners they need. ❖

Section Four: Putting the Lessons into Action

Chapter Twenty-Three:
Top 10 Content Marketing Lessons Learned from Successful Practitioners

1. Only content that is intrinsically valuable to your customers will work as a core component of your content marketing strategy.

2. You must have a thorough understanding of your customers and what is most important to them. If you do not understand the problems and challenges they face, you cannot hope to create content that is truly relevant to them. Without understanding their problems, you cannot provide solutions.

3. A comprehensive content marketing strategy may provide a complete or partial replacement of traditional advertising and marketing. Such a strategy can be both more effective and less expensive than doing things the old-fashioned way.

4. Print magazines can be a powerful weapon within your content marketing arsenal. They enable you to reach out with precision to your customers with carefully targeted messaging that is totally under your control.

5. Great design adds significant value to content marketing by making it more accessible, more appealing, and more actionable for your customers.

6. Your best content marketing investment may be in the creation of a dedicated internal or external team that understands how to produce great content and that lives and dies by the success of your content marketing program.

7. Drink your own Kool-Aid. Whenever possible, use your own company's products or services to prove their worth to your customers.

8. Get your customers to participate actively with the content you create in print and online. Begin a conversation and keep it going in order to earn their loyalty and trust.

9. Relevant and valuable content is just the first step in turning a prospect or visitor into a customer. You must then make it easy for them to buy.

10. Most of the best practices from the larger companies we profiled can be emulated in whole or in part even by very small organizations. It's not the money. It's the content marketing mindset that counts. Big ideas can trump big bucks.

Chapter Twenty-Four:
An In-Depth Case Study—Developing a Content Marketing Strategy from Start to Finish

The following is a fictitious case study base on real-life situations.

MODEL, Inc. creates software specifically for engineers who design manufactured products such as paint cans, plastic spray bottles, and even eyeglass frames. MODEL's software integrates with the larger design engineering software programs such as Autodesk's Inventor and Solid-Works (two very large, multi-national software companies), so MODEL's software is often bundled by these "affiliate" companies, wherein MODEL takes a cut.

MODEL's software focuses on 3D (three-dimensional) analysis. For years, MODEL had been fighting it out with two major competitors for the same customer base and was able to scrape a small market share with no direct sales representatives. It had a great product that was sold and distributed by two of the leading design software companies, which generated the majority of its business for the last five years.

Recently, MODEL has seen more competitors come into the market, which has taken away market share. In addition, MODEL has been hearing rumors that both Autodesk and SolidWorks, as well as other design engineering software companies, are planning on creating their own analysis software that would compete directly with theirs.

MODEL, a small 30-person firm with about $10 million in revenues, has an excellent core group of engineers and has been run by the same executive team since its launch in 1997. Unfortunately, MODEL has very low brand awareness in the industry, since it never had to market aggressively in the past. Many of its customers actually think the software it creates comes from Autodesk and Solid-Works, which both sell MODEL's software as an add-on product.

MODEL's executive team is freaking out. It has begun to invest in a sales force and customer service, but is concerned over what it can spend on marketing and, ultimately, how it should communicate with customers and prospects. What should this company do?

Positioning MODEL as Leaders in Analysis Software

Step One: Define the Organizational Goals.

The CEO called an off-site meeting to discuss the current situation. During that day, the team developed a renewed business plan that included some specific marketing goals. Among those were:

> » Build a robust website. This specifically meant acquiring 2,000 qualified names through its website efforts during the next year. MODEL believes it needs to close 5% of these corporate clients (100) in the next year (without the help of its design partners) to make an impact on the strategic goals of the company.

> » Be the name in "analysis." Executives believe that MODEL has the engineering excellence to be the "Intel Inside" of design analysis software. The measurement of this would be "the preferred brand name" when it came to analysis software within the next 12 months. MODEL is beginning the process with a benchmark study so it can clearly measure its increased awareness.

> » Sell direct to customers at least 50% of the time within 18 months. Currently, this number is 10%.

> » Keep the core base of users. Customer loyalty is key, so MODEL set customer renewal at 95% for the next year.

> » Double revenues over the next five years. An aggressive goal that it will meet through organic growth and possibly one key acquisition.

Step Two: Determine the Informational Needs of the Buyer.

Before doing anything, MODEL decided to talk to its core customers. It did this in two ways. First, the CEO and COO went out to see 20 customers and prospects face-to-face (some big, some small). In addition, MODEL conducted an online research study through Zoomerang that focused on not only what its customers and prospects thought, but what their informational needs were. In other words, what were the problems that kept its customers (design engineers) up at night?

The results of the research amazed the executive team. Here is what they found:

> » MODEL customers are very loyal. They love the software and often request it when moving to a new company or working with

outside partners.

» Newer MODEL customers did indeed think that MODEL software came from another company.

» Outside of MODEL customers, most design engineers had little awareness of MODEL or its software.

» Decisions about purchasing MODEL software were often made not by the design engineer, but by the owner or vice president of engineering.

» A top-three challenge among prospects was "analysis concerns." These prospects usually reached out to the larger software firms with questions on analysis, and not MODEL.

» Many design engineers were uneducated about analysis and weren't sure how to learn more about how it could help them in their jobs.

» Customers and prospects named MODEL as their preferred analysis brand only 7% of the time. There were seven other companies ahead of them, two of which did not create analysis software.

Step Three: Determine What You Want the Customer to Do and Why this Helps the Business.

Once MODEL executives completed steps one and two, step three seemed pretty easy to do. Here are some of the notes that the marketing team put together:

"We need some downloadable information so that we can get qualified design engineers' information to communicate with them on an ongoing basis."

"We need to create targeted marketing information for two groups: design engineers and C-level. Design engineers are both influencers and decision makers, depending on the size of the company. C-level executives are decision makers only and care about product quality, cost, and time-to-market. When either of these populations thinks about analysis, MODEL needs to be at the top of their list."

"We need engineers to try the product in some way…possibly offer a free trial of the software (MODEL does not offer a free trial at this time)."

Step Four: Determine the Product and Content Mix.

Armed with all of this information, MODEL executives sat in a half-day brainstorming meeting and created the following plan. They hired a facilitator to run the meeting, and also invited two key customers and an industry expert to participate (all three signed NDAs). Here is the plan they came up with:

Print Newsletter

The core of the content marketing initiative would be a 16-page print newsletter called *Design Analysis*. In order to differentiate this direct-mail initiative from other mail programs, MODEL decided to go with a digest-style, four-color format. *Design Analysis* would be mailed quarterly to a database of 10,000 customers and prospects already in the company's database (the same target as the research study), as well as an additional rented list of 15,000 design engineers from an industry publication. MODEL also decided to hold 2,000 customers/prospects out of the distribution to serve as a control group for measurement purposes. MODEL would integrate an opt-in strategy over the first nine months to enable customers and prospects to request the newsletter.

The marketing team worked with an audience development company to develop the final list size and target, determining that the final distribution would target 90% of MODEL's "model" company target. In companies larger than 100 employees, *Design Analysis* would be sent to at least three decision makers within the organization, including an engineering manager.

The content plan for the newsletter was simple: no selling, only educating. MODEL contracted with a leading freelance journalist to create the content plan for the newsletter, and with other freelancers from the industry to deliver the content. The ultimate goal was to position MODEL as *the* thought leader on analysis software. The publication was clearly marked as coming from MODEL, including one customer success story in each issue, and included a small ad on the mailing page of the issue.

Each article in the newsletter had multiple links to additional information on the MODEL website or other relevant websites. MODEL also made it easy for design engineers to sign up for the eNewsletter, including a clear subscription form on the MODEL home page and all content pages, a "forward to a friend" viral component, and a "widget" that customers and other engineers could use to feed in MODEL content on a daily basis.

eBook

The MODEL content team (made up of the MODEL marketing team

and a freelance editorial team) created *The Ultimate Survival Guide to Design Analysis*, a five-chapter eBook (about 60 pages) that would be promoted in every issue of the newsletter. The eBook would be free to download from the MODEL website, as long as the buyer completed some profile information.

The eBook would also be promoted via Pay-Per-Click (PPC) on Google and Yahoo!. The eBook would have one chapter promoted via a news release to: 1) help in search optimization efforts, and 2) attract the attention of industry bloggers and other influencers.

MODEL also bought text ads in key industry online newsletters to promote the eBook.

White Paper Series

In conjunction with each quarterly print newsletter, MODEL released a white paper on analysis targeted for senior-level engineers, VPs of engineering, and owners regarding the key benefits of analysis, such as time-to-market, product and process improvement, and cost savings during the manufacturing process.

Short abstracts of each white paper were promoted in the print newsletter. Each white paper was also promoted via a news release (multiple releases) and delivered to MODEL's opt-in management distribution e-file. MODEL also partnered with an industry media source to co-brand the white paper and promote each one to management.

All white papers were available for free to anyone who answered two, brief qualifying questions and provided their name, title, company, and e-mail address.

Finally, the white papers were promoted through a targeted PPC campaign and by contracting with a small SEO company that worked on organic placement of the white paper landing page.

The MODEL Website and Blog

Previously, the MODEL website was all product-oriented. Now, half of the homepage was taken up with consistent and relevant content from the above initiatives.

The biggest improvement was the launch of the *Design Analysis* blog, which was maintained by MODEL's engineering and technical support department. All six team members were given instructions to blog at least once per week, and were also responsible for five outside blogs and websites where they would become active in those blog communities by commenting and linking back to the MODEL blog.

The blog was registered with all major blog directories and Technorati, a blog search site. It focused on helpful analysis tips, short cuts, and industry trends. A news release was sent out after three months of blog posts announcing the blog to the industry.

Customer Facebook Fan Page

MODEL partnered with its top customers to create a customer Facebook group, where customers could share tips, tricks, and expertise through the social networking site. MODEL appointed two customers as co-moderators, as well as one of MODEL's engineers.

Article Marketing Program for Affiliates

In addition to its own content, MODEL created analysis articles for key affiliates in multiple industries about the benefits of analysis. This was done for free, as long as the article would cite MODEL as the source and link back to the MODEL website. MODEL's team also worked with a small public relations firm to help place modified articles where relevant and promoted the use of their content via Creative Commons Attribution 3.0 (http://creative-commons.org/licenses/by/3.0/).

News Releases

In addition to the news releases mentioned above, MODEL set up a news release calendar that included no fewer than two news releases per month. Eight out of 10 news releases had to contain educational content, while the other two were to be company announcements of some sort.

NOTE: Before any web launches, MODEL purchased 10 hours of an SEO expert's time to make sure that all web content would be properly tagged and indexed for search engines. It also used a search engine marketing expert to assist with keyword choices for the PPC eBook, in addition to the white paper program.

Final Step: Measuring the Program

Before any content initiatives were in place, MODEL took a snapshot of where it was, and then measured everything it could on a monthly basis. The following measurements were tracked:

Benchmark Study

At six months and one year from launch, MODEL repeated its initial benchmarking study against its control group. In the process, it also continued to get great ideas for its content through additional editorial questions.

Awareness levels and purchase intent were measured, both from design engineers and engineering management.

Web Statistics

MODEL tracked a number of web statistics, including:

- » Alexa.com rating
- » Blog RSS subscribers
- » Blog comments
- » Blog Technorati ranking
- » Print newsletter subscriptions
- » Unique site visitors
- » Unique site page views
- » Percentage of new visitors
- » Pages per visit
- » Google page rank
- » Top referrers
- » Top exit pages
- » White paper downloads
- » eBook downloads
- » Most popular pages

Sales-Related Statistics

The marketing team measured conversions of eBook downloads to sales and pipeline, white paper conversions, and print subscription conversions. Also, measurements were analyzed between those who just signed-up for the free trial vs. those who signed-up and also downloaded an additional, or multiple, content products.

Current customers who downloaded content products were compared against current customers who did not download any products. MODEL found that customers who downloaded or subscribed to a content product had a 20% better retention rate and purchased an average of 1.2 additional products.

In Summary

By looking at marketing through the lens of content marketing, MODEL, Inc. was able to outperform in a highly competitive environment. Previously, MODEL didn't see marketing as important because it didn't have to market to survive and, truthfully, didn't understand it. Today, MODEL's entire marketing plan is about making its customers smarter, which is not only more fun to implement, it works better than anything else they could have executed. ❖

Chapter Twenty-Five:
Marketing Survival

When you began reading this book, you were probably a skeptic about the content marketing revolution. Frankly, five years ago we were pretty much traditional marketers ourselves. Today, we are unapologetic content marketing evangelists.

That's why we have written *Get Content. Get Customers*. We are compelled to share the lessons that we have learned as media executives, as observers of content marketing best practices, and, ultimately, as content marketing practitioners ourselves. Of course, as you have certainly realized by now, this book is part of our own content marketing strategy.

Although most organizations still rely primarily, if not exclusively, on traditional marketing tactics, a rapidly growing number of companies of all sizes are proving that content marketing is the one strategy that will pay dividends for their customers and for themselves.

In fact, the accelerating shift to content marketing is occurring not because it's fashionable, but because it's effective.

Smart marketers around the globe are using the concepts from this book to create customer-focused, innovative organizations. Bottom-line-driven multi-nationals are moving mega-bucks from traditional media to content marketing initiatives because it drives both sales and profitability.

Moreover, many practitioners have been able to eliminate traditional marketing strategies altogether. In fact, as we've written, even very traditional companies have successfully deployed content marketing strategies in print, online, and in person.

You now understand that the transformation from traditional to content marketing often requires both a new mindset and a new skill set. Although that's easier to say than to do, we are convinced that you and your team must make that transformation.

You may be concerned about the risks of making dramatic changes in your approach to marketing within your organization. We urge you to concentrate instead on the risks inherent in failing to make the changes necessary to compete for the new breed of buyer. We all know that many otherwise-smart companies remain mired in prehistoric marketing methodologies. If you're hesitating, think once again about the fate of the dinosaurs.

We don't know what caused the dinosaurs' demise eons ago. But, when it comes to the demise of marketing dinosaurs in the twenty-first century, we know for sure what will kill them off: the failure to develop and deploy successful content marketing strategies in the face of a game-changing metamorphosis in the business environment.

Don't be a marketing dinosaur. Start implementing your content marketing strategy today, and, as they say over at Nike, "Just do it." ❖

Acknowledgements

There are countless people and organizations that made this book possible. Special thanks to our editor Lisa Murton Beets and to Mike Azzara and David Drickhamer who showed us some tough editing love. These three individuals gave us the greatest gift we could have imagined: They told us when we were wrong. Thanks to each of you for your guidance and expertise.

Thanks to those people who opened the door to our many interviews and provided core information about the content marketing process, especially (in alphabetical order) Gail Anderson, Lisa Arthur, Mike Azzara, Bob Bloom, Judy Bricker, Mary Briggs, Chris Carson, Linda Cleary, Katie Coletto, Marie Kroesen Connell, Katie Danforth, Stephanie Diamond, Chris Elliott, Carlos Fernandes, Paul Gerbbino, Brett Gilbertson, Eric Groves, Eric Holter, Barry Judge, April Kettelle, Pam Kozelka, Jennifer LeClaire, Michael Linenberger, Gaelen O'Connell, Carol Orsborn, Ann Porter, Mike Reagan, Kamilla Reid, Vickie Reiner, Tonia Ries, Linda Rigano, Struan Robertson, Rebecca Rolfes, John Sprecher, David Strom, Melinda Venable, and Mitch York.

A final thanks to those who influenced us and this book along the way, including (in no particular order) Don Schultz, David Meerman Scott, Seth Godin, Stephanie Diamond, Paul Gillin, Rohit Barghava, Jim McDermott, Angela Vannucci, Simon Kelly, Ardath Albee, Peter Banks, Christian Coughlan, Kenneth Kessler, Ian Alexander, Hans de Keulenaer, Paul Conley, Chuck Francisco, Rex Hammock, Bob Rosenbaum, Michael Hurley, Aaron Kahlow, Greg Kiskadden, Benson Lee, Scott Owen, Glenn Sabin, Jim Meyers, Eric Schneider, Jeremy Morris, Glenn Nicholas, Jim O'Hare, Janet Robbins, Jackie Ross, Antoinette DeJohn, and Patrick Schaber.

From Newt Barrett

My wonderful wife, Maxine, has been the perfect partner in work and in life. Through all my professional highs and lows, she has kept me centered and motivated to keep doing the work that I love. Her gifts of laughter and love bring joy to all around her. Thank you, Maxine, for everything.

My joyous gratitude also goes to my extended family, from my wonderful sisters, Dibbie and Susan, to an awesome clan of aunts, uncles, and cousins who collectively possess the planet's most wonderful sense of humor. They have made even the bad times seem like good times.

I've been very lucky in my life to have made friends and colleagues that I cherished even in jobs that I hated. I have been further blessed to experience a series of golden moments where great colleagues, great work, and great companies came together all at once. My thanks go to all those colleagues and friends who enabled me to achieve a level of success that I never could have imagined as a kid growing up in Cleveland, Ohio. Together, we accomplished a lot, laughing all the while. It just doesn't get any better than that.

Finally, to my co-author, Joe Pulizzi, thank you for including me on this wonderful literary adventure. Let's do it again—just not too soon.

From Joe Pulizzi

To me, a book seems like the culmination of two things: the people I've met and known, and the books and blogs I've read. I could literally go on for pages about all the people who have positively affected me to this point in my life and my career. That said, this short list contains the people who, in their own way, have done something truly remarkable, which I take with me each day. I wish I had room for more.

To my wife Pam, my partner in all things. From you I learned how to be a better man, a better husband, and a better father, and what it really means to be successful. All my love.

To my son Joshua. From you I learned that a man is a success when he is loved by a child. Always remember that it is not the biggest or strongest or fastest who win, but the one with the most heart.

To my son Adam. From you I learned that God comes in the form of a smile, a hug, or a laugh. Heed the words of Yoda, "Do or do not...there is no try."

To Tony and Terry, my parents. From you I learned faith, true love, and unselfishness. Thanks for always being there for me.

To the late F. Leo Groff, my grandfather. From you I learned that the smallest action can literally change the course of someone's future.

To James McDermott, my mentor. From you I learned in the value of a process, that execution is what counts, and that playing it safe can be the biggest risk of all.

To Newt Barrett, my co-author. From you I learned dedication and the ability to execute, even with no available time. You are an inspiration.

Philippians 4:13

Index

About the Authors

Joe Pulizzi is founder and chief content officer for Junta42, the leading online resource dedicated to content marketing. Junta42's Match is the industry's only online marketplace for content marketing and custom publishing solutions. Pulizzi is also president for Z Squared Media, LLC, a content marketing consulting firm. A nationally recognized expert and speaker in online content marketing and social media, Pulizzi serves on the board for the Custom Publishing Council, two-time chairperson for American Business Media, and served as vice president for Penton Media, overseeing their custom media operation. He has been recognized for dozens of awards in and around content marketing, including Cleveland 20/30's Top Mover and Shaker under 35.

Newt Barrett is president of Content Marketing Strategies, a division of Voyager Media, Inc. Content Marketing Strategies helps small- and medium-sized companies attract new customers through the use of relevant content practices. Barrett is also founder of ContentMarketingToday.com, an educational website dedicated to helping marketers find new ways to reach their customers in print, online, and in-person. Barrett is a successful publishing executive with more than 25 years of experience, launching publications for CMP, Ziff-Davis, Penton Media, Inc., and Southwest Florida Business. Barrett currently serves on the board of the Southwest Florida Leadership Foundation.

For more information, please visit www.getcontentgetcustomers.com

More of Joe at blog.junta42.com

More of Newt at www.ContentMarketing.net

Printed in the United States
117122LV00001B/4/P

9 780980 187809